Of
Marketing
and
Emasculated
Goats

Advertising and Marketing
Insights from the Oddest Places

———

Steve Cuno

Goat illustration (modified) courtesy of pixabay.com

ISBN-13: 978-1530913688
ISBN-10: 1530913683

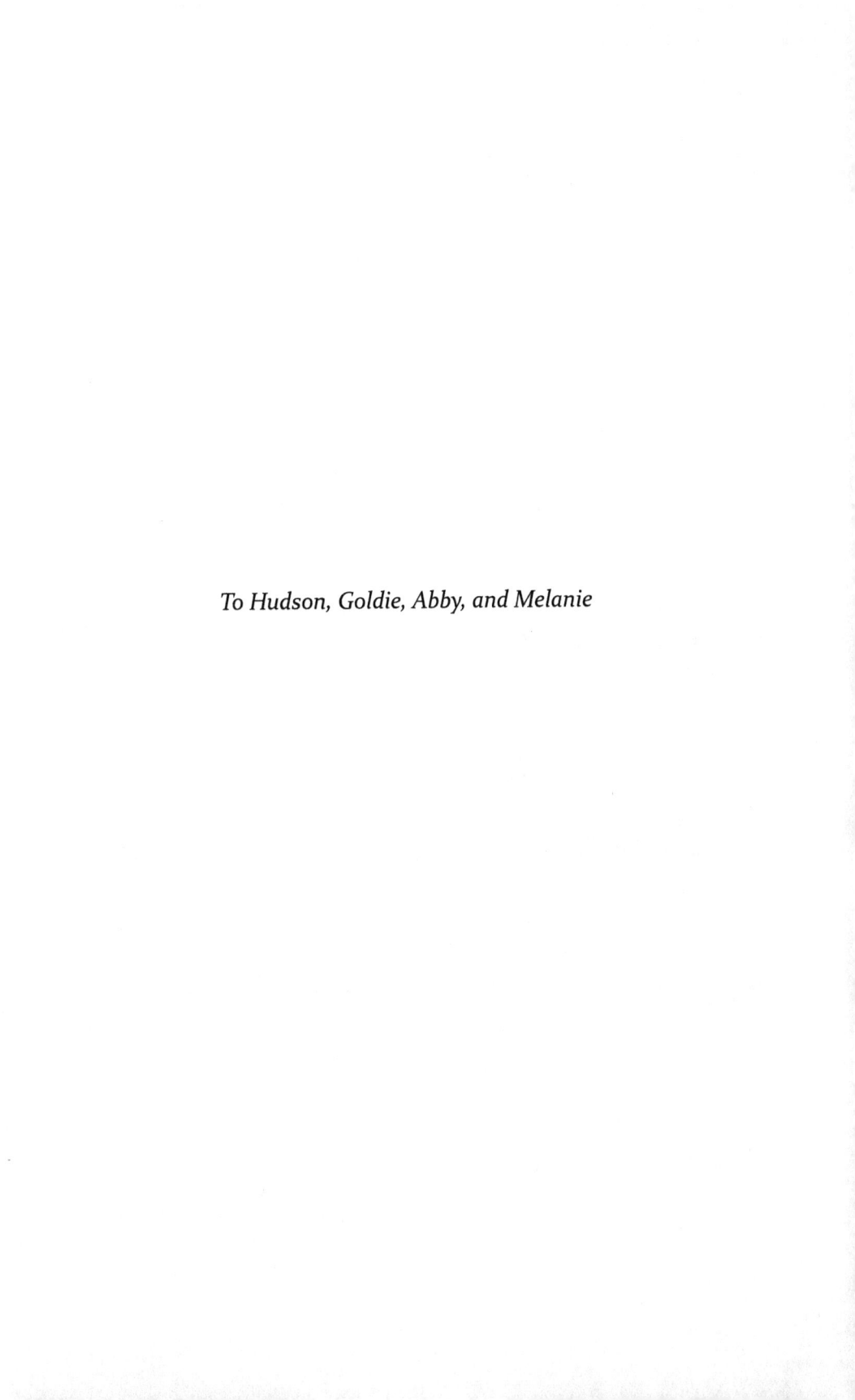

To Hudson, Goldie, Abby, and Melanie

Contents

Foreword

Getting to Know Your Inner Goat

Early 20th century Milford, Kansas, was not the best place to be a man looking to enhance his virility. It was, however, better than being a goat. Most of the men and all of the goats who arrived in Milford for a certain procedure at the hands of medical quack John R. Brinkley left quite dead. Incredibly, Brinkley's practice flourished anyway.

Brinkley's steady stream of patients despite greater than 50 percent odds of death provided the inspiration for Chapter 1, from which this volume takes its title. It was originally published in article form by *MarketingProfs.com*. Other online and print periodicals with no better sense than to have published me over the course of my career include *Deliver, Skeptical Inquirer, Adnews, Business Connect, BookBusiness, Swift, Digital IQ,* and *Inside Direct.*

The inspiration for this compilation came when I was looking through my articles and thought, "Maybe if I edited and updated this stuff, it would make for a decent book." Here I beg your indulgence: Since each chapter began life as a solo article, some of my points and examples make more than one appearance.

I hope that you enjoy reading, and that you emerge eager to do more creative, more profitable, more ethical work.

Steve Cuno
Salt Lake City

Introduction

Why Do Advertising Gurus Recycle the Same Old Pap?

This morning I clicked on an article promising to reveal the secrets of successful advertising. It disappointed. The "secrets" turned out to be the usual banalities like "you have to stand out" and "present your product's advantages." Anyone with the IQ of a spaghetti squash could produce a better list, and do it without the help of a guru.

I would find it less disturbing were the article unique. It is not. The advertising trade press publishes many such embarrassments and passes them off as vital insights.

Why do we hold up as "gurus" and "consultants" those who regurgitate the tired, the mundane, the obvious? Why does no one stand up and yell, "Hey! How about something to broaden our horizons, add to our skills, make us rethink our approach, make us angry, and maybe even make us better at our jobs?"

I am not challenging the importance of fundamentals. I review some of them in this book. I'm challenging the practice of bestowing guru status upon people who foist clichés and platitudes as "insights." To be sure, there are useful gurus, but they are fewer in number, less famous, and a lot less rich than their platitude-spinning counterparts.

I suspect that there are two reasons that shallow, platitudinous gurus exist in greater number and make a whole lot more money.

Suspected Reason 1: No one likes a consultant who tells you that you're doing things wrong. Unless, that is, "doing things wrong" means "not realizing how great you are and doing more of it." Show advertising people why their award-winning work lacks selling power and you can kiss your guru career goodbye. Tell them that they have a certain *je ne sais quoi*, that they have a rare, intuitive gift for recognizing great work when they see it, and that anyone who objects just doesn't get it, and they will buy your books and pay you to give keynotes at conventions.

I used to teach a two-day seminar on predictive advertising methods for the Direct Marketing Association. In New York, after I had challenged typical pre-research methods and suggested better ones, the creative director of a sizable agency made this revealing remark: "You want us to go back and tell management and clients to change our research methods? It's not going to happen." Note that he didn't question what I'd presented. Rather, he made a telling observation about egos and the course of least resistance. The agency's fiduciary responsibility to give the client its most effective work would have to take a back seat.

Change requires humility followed by effort. It's much easier and way more romantic to stay the course and dismiss challenges as torpedoes to be damned.

To be fair, the don't-make-me-change frame of mind is human nature. Marketers have no exclusive right to it, but neither are we immune.

Suspected Reason 2: The few times I have visited with alleged gurus, I have been surprised at how little substance many of them have in the first place. Not a few have built their careers on gathering and repeating the clichés and platitudes on which *other* alleged gurus have built *their* careers.

Yet they are not to be blamed, for in fact it is our fault. These "gurus" deliver no more nor less than what We The Market demand. See *Suspected Reason 1.*

I have spent my career trying to escape that trap. I hope that this book inspires a reader or two to eschew the easy path and stubbornly cling to knowing and doing what works. If you do, you'll earn a greater return for your clients, but you'll never become a guru.

Author's Note

What I Mean by "Direct Response"

Please do not assume that *direct response marketing*, to which I often refer in these pages, means *direct mail*. *Direct mail* is a medium, just as the Internet, TV, radio, newspapers, magazines, and billboards are media. All of these, not just mail, are suitable for *direct response*.

When I talk about *direct response marketing*, or *direct response* or *direct marketing* for short, I'm referring to the practice of getting the market to respond promptly and *directly* to the advertiser, regardless of the medium. When I'm talking specifically about *direct mail*, I make it clear.

Direct response advertising differs considerably from advertising that seeks to build *brand awareness*. For that reason, marketing firms tend to specialize in one or the other. Those claiming to be skilled in both are usually kidding themselves.

I kind of set myself up there. As you'll see, I claim to be skilled in both. Decide if you will that I, too, am kidding myself; as long as you promise not to confuse direct response marketing et al for direct mail, I'll be happy.

Part One

Marketing Lessons From Critters

Chapter 1

Of Marketing and Emasculated Goats

There was no Viagra in 1918, but there were plenty of goats.

At the time, the alleged sexual prowess of goats enjoyed legendary status. So it was that Kansas physician John R. Brinkley made a small fortune by surgically implanting goat testicles in men seeking to enhance or restore their virility. Never mind that the procedure failed to deliver the promised benefit, that Brinkley was a medical school dropout who bought a diploma for $100, or that most of his patients died during or shortly after surgery. A steady supply of men handed over their cash to Brinkley's scruples and their privates to his scalpel.

I hope you agree that the decision to undergo Brinkley's procedure was irrational. The risks of infection, mutilation, sterility, and death were clear. There was no evidence that the men lucky enough to survive Brinkley's knife walked away any more virile than when they arrived. Yet presumably intelligent men convinced themselves to go ahead with implantation anyway. Why?

Of course, you know the answer. People who really, *really* want to believe something *will* believe it, regardless of where evidence points. Brinkley's patients really, *really* wanted to believe that his procedure would deliver the promised benefit, so they embraced his trumped-up "success stories" and disqualified all evidence to the contrary.

A century later, we haven't changed much. Consider the people you know who set aside evidence and common sense in favor of staying in bad relationships, racking up charges on psychic hotlines, lending money to losers, or wearing magnets to ward off arthritis, all motivated by an acute desire to believe.

Or, consider marketers who believe that their programs are working, even when evidence says otherwise or, more often, when there is no evidence at all.

Do you make irrational leaps in marketing?

All people, even marketers, are subject to irrational thinking. It's not a question of how smart you are, but of having evolved in an environment where certain impulsive actions helped keep us alive. Hunter-gatherers who paused to investigate whether a nearby roar signaled a hungry lioness or a mischievous parrot didn't last as long as those who simply ran. Indeed, magnetic resonance brain imaging indicates that we are wired to believe the first possibility that enters our head. Taking a rational, second look isn't instinctive. It's something we must train ourselves to do.

Much of today's marketing works, but a good deal more has little or no effect, and some of it actually drives sales down. That much shouldn't surprise anyone who understands bell curves. What is surprising is how few marketers have a clue as to where on the bell curve their marketing falls. This is not to imply that most marketers willfully deceive. Many have simply and unwittingly embraced time-honored marketing myths. The myths are usually based on leaps that someone made long ago without checking for parrots.

Here are six out of many possible examples.

Irrational Leap #1: "Everyone knows..."

Bad ideas are often embraced—and good ones often dismissed—thanks to what "everyone" knows. "Everyone knows" that no one reads long ads, watches late-night TV, or buys when they sense that you're "trying to sell them something." So marketers keep copy under 100 words, spend a fortune on Prime Time, and sacrifice sales to subtlety. Trouble is, these are cases in which "everyone" is mistaken. Long copy outsells short, advertising on late-night TV generates more orders than on Prime Time, and blatantly promotional advertising outsells advertising that holds back.

Given how often "everyone" is right, deference is understandable. Everyone knows—and rightly so—not to play catch with a hornet's nest, stick a finger in a fan, or pick on someone bigger that one's own size. But on the other hand, not too long ago "everyone" knew that our planet was stationary, time was constant, stress caused ulcers, and Iraq was stockpiling WMDs.

Marketing is rife with what "everyone knows" that turns out not to be so. Some of marketing's most prevalent and damaging myths are "my gut is always right," "focus groups are predictive," "awareness means success," "sales are up because of the ads," and "award-winning advertising is effective." These happen to be the subjects of Leaps 2 through 6.

Irrational Leap #2: "My tummy tells me..."

Raise your hand—or just roll your eyes—if your boss ever embraced a bad idea or rejected a good one with, "I'm going with my gut on this one, and my gut is never wrong."

It's doubtful that anyone's gut intuition is right even most of the time. More often, hindsight bias tricks people into remembering times when the lower half's prognostications panned out and overlooking times when they didn't. Hindsight bias aside, there is the problem of managed feedback. Many an employee, fearful of Shot Messenger Syndrome, will validate the boss's intuition with a steady stream of positive reports, factual or not.

The fact is, every restaurant that went under, every movie that failed, every new product that languished on the clearance rack, and every business venture that capsized started out with the full endorsement of someone's gut.

Irrational Leap #3: "Research shows..."

If you show storyboards to groups of 10 to 20 people who say, "That commercial would make me buy," you have a winner, right? If you phone 5,000 people and 80% say they'll switch to your brand thanks to your new tagline, they will, right?

Nope. Focus group participants told Telebrands CEO A. J. Kubani that they would cheerfully pay $19.95 for his Robo-Maid product. But when he opened up a trunk of ready-to-purchase RoboMaids, not one of them bought. And you may remember from your high school American history class that both the Roper and Gallup organizations predicted a win for Dewey in the 1948 presidential race. In case you missed it, Truman won.

Such cases are not unusual. If you ask people what they do, why they do it, or what they think they would do in a hypothetical situation, you'll learn much about their self-concept and little to nothing about their behavior. Don't believe me? Ask people—even in an anonymous survey—how often they wash after using the restroom. Then hide in a stall and count how many actually do. The difference between what people believe they will do (or not do) and what you observe them do (or not do) will surprise you. It may also discourage you from ever accepting another handshake.

Irrational Leap #4: "Awareness is up..."

Advertising was invented to deliver a pitch in place of a live salesperson. Its measure of success was the number of people who purchased. Later, advertisers began judging their work by the number of people who noticed or remembered a campaign. Today, many advertisers believe that an ad has "done its job" if it has drawn notice. To put this silly notion to the test, think about the Taco Bell Chihuahua, Ford Edsel, New Coke, Wendy's pigtail-wig, Alka-Seltzer's "I can't believe I ate the whole thing," and "Joe Isuzu." All of them failed but to this day enjoy top-of-mind awareness.

Irrational Leap #5: "Sales are up..."

It sounds convincing to say, "Sales went up when we ran the ads, so the campaign worked." Unfortunately, that line of reasoning is based on a logical fallacy well enough known to have its own Latin name: *Post hoc, ergo propter hoc.* "After this, therefore because of this."

It's an easy leap to make, since what happens first often *does* cause what happens next. If you experience indigestion after overeating, you can safely blame the overeating. But despite what positive mental attitude gurus preach, coincidences happen all the time, and they have the power to fool us. In the early 1980s, sagging Harley-Davidson sales picked up at about the same time the company cranked up the creativity of its advertising. So the new ad campaign obviously caused the sales increase—or did it? Also at the same time, President Reagan increased the tariff on imported motorcycles from 4.4% to 49.4%. Maybe that had something to do with the company's sales turnaround.

Do not be embarrassed if you have fallen for *Post hoc, ergo propter hoc.* You may feel better knowing that some fools actually claim that what happens *after* can retroactively cause what happened *before*. Try wrapping your mind around *that*.

If sales surged in the wake of your marketing campaign, congratulations are in order. But you'll need more than a correlation to establish that the campaign caused it.

Irrational Leap #6: "It won lots of awards..."

A look at advertising award competitions reveals categories like "Best Photography," "Best Use of Humor," "Best Design," "Best Original Score," "Best Copy," and "Best Directing." Everything, it seems, except "Sold the Most Widgets."

Funny thing. Awards given to salespeople are tied to numbers. I bet you've never seen a salesperson receive an award for funniest pitch, best jingle, or most original attire.

If you want to prove that awards are synonymous with marketing success, you'll need to exclude from your data: straightforward ads, like those for household products, that produce sales; corny ads, like those for ShamWow, that make fortunes; and highly-praised creative ads, like the Taco Bell Chihuahua, that fail to increase sales.

Or, you could just admit that awards are great for the ego. There's nothing wrong with having an ego, nor with boosting it with awards, as long as you keep things in perspective.

Toward rational marketing

You needn't be subject to irrational leaps. Here are some tips for making rational marketing decisions.

Conduct a valid predictive test. The trick is to quit asking people to *tell* you their behavior and get them to unwittingly *show* you their behavior instead. How do you suppose the retail industry learned that people in the U.S. tend to move to their right upon entering a store? Hint: not by asking them in focus groups or phone surveys. Researchers hid in stores and watched.

There are many ways to put customers in a position to show you how they'll behave. All it takes is a little imagination. Say you want to choose between Headline A and Headline B. Create two websites or mailers that are identical but for the headline. Be sure to include a free incentive offer. Now, expose one half of a valid market sample to Headline A and the other half to Headline B. Whatever you do, do not tell either group that you're testing, and do not ask them to tell you what they think. Don't even let them know you're paying attention. Just count the clicks or replies. You can be pretty sure that whichever headline pulls more clicks or replies is the stronger one. To be more than just pretty sure, retest. If you get the same results, the evidence is that you're on solid ground.

Take the emotion out of your decisions. The passion to be right is intoxicating. Sober up. Your objective is to sell widgets, not to bolster your ego. As you design a valid test, resolve in advance to accept the results, even if they fail to support your hunches.

Maintain control groups as a matter of policy. A sales increase during a campaign might or might not be due to coincidence. You can find out by establishing a control group, a representative sample of customers who aren't exposed to your campaign. A quick comparison of a control group's versus other customers' purchases will tell you what effect, if any, your campaign had.

Resist the urge to jump to conclusions. Logic leaps are beguiling. Familiarize yourself with common logical fallacies and learn to avoid them. Force yourself to collect valid evidence. Remain open to what the evidence says, and skeptical of what you wish it to say.

Warding off bean counters

The more you train yourself to eschew unwarranted leaps, the more you will approach marketing from a sober, rational standpoint. You will find yourself creating and refining campaigns that are demonstrably and measurably successful.

Then, next time a bean counter turns a greedy eye on your budget, you won't have to defend your work with dodges like, "but it's so creative," "it won an award," "it did well in focus groups," and "I feel in my gut that it works." The numbers will speak for themselves.

It's too late to save Brinkley's patients. I'm afraid it's also too late for the goats. It's not too late for marketers.

Chapter 2

Marketing and the Sexual Preferences of Finches

Female zebra finches dig male zebra finches in red hats. This we know thanks to evolutionary biologist Nancy Burley who, quite by accident, discovered that red bands affixed to the legs of male zebra finches seemed to arouse considerable passion in the females. Blue-banded males fared less well but better than their green-banded buddies, who fared poorly.

Intrigued, Burley fashioned tiny paper hats and glued them to the heads of randomly chosen males. The females liked the hats even more than they liked the bands. Once again, red hats proved most popular, followed by blue. One cannot help feeling bad for the males who received green hats.

It appears that natural selection, as it seems to have done for peahens, has resulted in female finches attracted to taller, more brightly colored males. Before we shake our heads in bafflement, consider that we humans are not so different. We judge not just potential mates but job applicants, consultants, salespeople, and even friends by the cut of a suit, the quality of a strip of silk tied about the neck, the price of a car, a haircut, accent, height, posture, and other differences that may not necessarily speak directly to quality.

We judge products that way, too. A product showcased in attractive packaging inspires greater confidence than the same product in a plain wrapper. Wine experts are more likely to extoll the taste of a wine in a bottle with a high price tag. Audiophiles pay a premium for gold-plated cables, even though ordinary cables deliver the same signal. People pay more for purified spring water than for chemically identical purified tap water and swear they can taste a difference. Purebred dogs sell for thousands while virtually identical pedigree-less dogs are offered free to good homes. Health-conscious consumers pay more for natural and organic foods, unaware that no significant health advantage has been established, or that "natural" and "organic" do not always mean what they think.

It's not unusual for brands to take advantage of this proclivity. People who pay dearly for a Mont Blanc or a Rolex are careless or doubtful that a Bic or Timex gets the same job done. There need be no apparent difference in quality for Victoria's Secret to charge many times more than Sears for lingerie. An otherwise unremarkable sweater becomes a thing of greater value when adorned with a Louis Vuitton logo.

Still, capricious ornamentation has its limits. Should you wear a little red hat to a singles bar, do not be surprised if you leave as alone as when you arrived.

Chapter 3

What My Dog Taught Me About Marketing

f you have spent more than three seconds with a dog, you probably know Fido's Law: $s=w^2$. It's shorthand for the well-established scientific fact that a dog's slobber production equals the square of its body weight.

No wonder, then, that one evening as my guests tried to appear not to mind my German Shepherd slobbering on them, I felt it was my moral duty to say, "Abby, go to your place." Without hesitation, Abby turned from the guests, crossed the room to her doggy bed, and lay down.

I would love tell you that I acted purely out of courtesy for my guests, but I am smaller than that. I was showing off. I knew that two of the couples present owned unruly dogs. Seeing their jaws drop at Abby's obedience was the high point of my evening.

Heady as showing off is, training dogs has brought me another benefit. Sound dog training principles are not so different from those of good marketing. Both deal with using common sense, communication, observation, and mutual respect to motivate desired behaviors in social creatures. Here are four lessons we marketers might pick up from our best friend.

Lesson One: Clarity never faileth. Well-trained dogs weren't born knowing voice commands. A good trainer helps them understand what they're expected to do. One method for teaching a dog to come when called, for instance, is to attach a 20-foot leash to the collar, call the dog, gently reel in the leash, and praise the dog when it reaches you. Your dog will soon figure out that "Here, Rover" means "Here, Rover."

Likewise, don't expect people exposed to your advertising to know what you want them to do. If you want them to click a link, call a toll-free number, bring in a coupon, or visit a store, tell them in a way that they can't miss. A bright blue link that says "get more information by clicking here" is the marketing equivalent of a 20-foot leash, pulling wandering readers to the desired action.

Lesson Two: Reward positive behavior. Dogs are too smart to do something for nothing. Some require treats, some settle for praise, but all need a reward or incentive of some sort.

So do people. Whether for small or big-ticket items, a compelling incentive will multiply response. I doubled natural gas fireplace sales by offering a free jar of honey for visiting a showroom. The jar of honey, incidentally, retailed for only one dollar. For an industrial manufacturer, I tripled sales by offering a $20 Victoria's Secret gift certificate. Even though (or perhaps because) most of that client's customers were male.

Lesson Three: No one likes to miss out. My yellow Labrador Tucker has no interest in wasting his time letting me pet him. Unless, that is, I start petting Abby. In that case, Tucker appears from nowhere and shoves Abby out of the way.

Psychological tests show that humans, like dogs, are more often motivated by the prospect of missing out than of gaining. In one study, people reported that they'd rather be the only person in a room to win $100 than to win $150 with the knowledge that someone else in the room just won $1,000. In other words, they would give up $50 to avoid feeling outdone.

Marketers can use this insight to their advantage. A power utility's message saying people would *lose* money if they *didn't* respond generated more response than one saying they'd *save* money if they *did* respond. A respected international business magazine increased subscription revenues by making *not* taking a higher-priced option look like a missed opportunity.

Lesson Four: Treat them well, and they will be loyal. The nicer you are, the more willingly your dog comes when called, protects your home from intruders, and resists the urge to chew shoes that you happen to leave out. But even a well-trained dog isn't above a little revenge if you are unkind. Abby would sooner have exploded than soil my house. But when an ill-behaved teenager stayed with us for a short time, Abby managed to find and profane the lad's personal belongings on a daily basis. (Dare I confess? I was pleased.)

When you treat customers well—keep promises, back up products, maintain a generous return policy, hire courteous people—they tend to reward you with repeat business. They'll even overlook the occasional slip. But let them down too often, and they will do worse than profane your belongings. The days when complaints from dissatisfied customers reached only 200 people are long gone. Today a single customer complaint can go viral and create worldwide infamy in minutes.

Bonus Lesson: Don't take the analogy too far. We have much to learn from our best friend, but let's not go overboard. If you find yourself in trouble for scratching your ear with your foot, howling when you hear an ambulance, chasing cats, rolling around on a pile of rotting leaves, or marking your territory, don't blame me, and don't tell the judge it was my idea.

Chapter 4

A Call to Action, Labrador Retriever-Style

I n Chapter 3, I introduced you to Tucker, the Labrador retriever with more important things to do than stand around while I pet him. His highest priority is to ensure that no leaf blows past my front window without my hearing from him loud and clear.

But if he spies me petting Abby, who happens to be my other dog and therefore his competition, he will abandon his window post and insinuate himself between us.

Such behavior isn't unique to canines.

Psychologists and behavioral economists have long known that social creatures, which dogs and humans happen to be, are often *less* motivated by the prospect of gain, and *more* motivated by the fear of missing out on what others may gain.

The principle is no mere theorist's plaything. If you don't believe me, try singling out from a group one child to receive a treat or one employee to receive a special privilege. Mayhem is sure to ensue.

The tendency not to want to miss out finds real-world application in marketing. When an electronics retailer presented small and midsize TVs for sale, consumers usually opted for the smaller model. No surprise there—the midsize model cost 23 percent more. But when he added a large model priced 74 percent higher than the midsize model, people began trading up from the small to the midsize model. It seems that a 74 percent price hike made a 23 percent hike look like a bargain not to be missed.

Some marketers have a hard time wrapping their minds around selling the avoidance of regret. It seems counter-intuitive, possibly even blasphemous. Maybe that's because ever since Dr. Norman Vincent Peale penned *The Power of Positive Thinking*, motivational speakers have been badgering us to banish from our minds all but the most positive thoughts and words. Clearly, Peale never played with TV prices.

We humans are a competitive lot. Like horses that set out on a friendly, side-by-side trot and end up racing each other, we hate to be outdone. In one study, more people said they would rather earn $50,000 a year and live in a neighborhood where everyone else makes $25,000 a year than earn $100,000 a year where the neighbors earn $250,000. They would give up $50,000 in annual income to be the highest paid on the block. H. L. Mencken wasn't altogether rhetorical when he said, "A wealthy man is one who earns $100 a year more than his wife's sister's husband."

I had my doubts about that. Until, that is, one of my employees told me about his Texas lottery win. Upon learning that he had chosen five out of six winning numbers, he supposed that he had won tens of thousands of dollars. But as luck had it, several other people had also picked five out of six winning numbers, lowering his take to $700. Friends congratulated him on his win, but he was furious at not having won more.

Loyalty marketers prove this principle all the time. It's well known in the loyalty industry that free gift offers motivate new customers to join loyalty programs. But what is less known is that higher-end, established customers are more motivated by *privileges that are unavailable to the masses.* Accruing frequent flier miles toward a free trip is all well and good, but executive-level travelers *love* skipping the long check-in line in full view of the less privileged. The same strategy underlies the success of tactics such as private invitation sales, preferred customer seating, and personal recognition from a CEO.

That's why time-limited incentive offers increase the selling power of advertisements many times over. The idea of "I will miss out on this free offer if I don't buy now" motivates prompt action.

The "don't miss out" strategy must be crafted with finesse, and it is not to be overused. It is still important to sell benefits. But if you can weave in the threat of potential discontent for those who hesitate, perhaps a few more customers, like Tucker, will take action.

Chapter 5

A Lesson From Your Friendly Neighborhood Vampire Bat

By the time I finished college, I had worked in succession for three major department store chains. Not that you asked, but I sold shoes and, later, carpets. Each of the chains claimed to have originated the policy, "Satisfaction guaranteed or your money back." They also alleged that naysayers shook their heads at the guarantee, predicting widespread abuse sure to bankrupt them in no time. But—cue orchestra and heavenly choir—these courageous retail pioneers damned the torpedoes and moved ahead at full speed.

If the folklore is true, history vindicated the pioneers. Today, a satisfaction guarantee is standard for nearly all retail, online, and mail order marketers. Customers who abuse the privilege are inevitable, but increased sales more than compensate. It seems that when stores trust customers, customers trust stores, become loyal, and show it by purchasing more.

If the guarantee's positive outcome surprised naysayers, one thing is clear. Naysayers in those days didn't spend much time with vampire bats.

After feeding upon sleeping cattle or some other creature snoozing blissfully away, vampire bats regroup at headquarters, regurgitate their spoils, and share equally. But even bats are subject to greed. Should a successful hunter hoard instead of share, the others notice. Next time that bat experiences a bad hunt, it will be excluded from the sharing.

If you think that these bats appear to observe some sort of innate code, including punishing violators by shunning them, you would be right. Innate codes of conduct in social animals like bats—and humans—have important implications for marketers hoping to win loyalty.

You and I might call the bat behavior a primitive version of, "Scratch my back and I'll scratch yours; don't scratch my back and I'll be damned if I'll scratch yours." Evolutionary psychologists call it *reciprocal altruism,* which sounds way more intellectual than "mutual back-scratching." The trait shows up in most creatures that live in social groups. Dolphins instinctively protect the young and disabled from sharks. Wolves and wild dogs naturally slip into strict hierarchical rules of feeding, mating, and pack safety. Chimpanzees practice hauntingly human-like politics. In all of these species, compliance to the "rules" leads to rewards, whereas flouting them incurs penalties. Indeed, chimp punishment sometimes entails biting off parts most creatures prefer to keep. Vampire bats go easy on miscreants by comparison.

While to a certain degree reciprocal altruism can be learned, evidence suggests that it is for the most part as innate in bats, dolphins, wolves, and chimps as echolocation, surfacing for air, marking territory, and climbing trees.

If a sense of fairness is innate in so-called lower creatures, what about humans? Is it possible that our own sense of justice runs deeper than what society instills?

Studies of primitive and modern societies by scientists like Jared Diamond and Napoleon Chagnon indicate that the answer is a strong YES. An inner, tacit understanding of how we should relate to and treat one another appears to come as naturally to humans as talking with our hands.

If that's true, then a positive response to a marketer who is willing to go out on a limb for customers may not be so surprising after all. Maybe it's simply natural.

No wonder "satisfaction guaranteed" has become a must for successful marketing. When you scratch a shopper's back, it's natural for the shopper to scratch in return. When a high-end online or retail clothier gives you a no-hassle refund because your outfit "just didn't look right" even after you wore it, you're more inclined to reward the behavior with increased loyalty, purchases, and referrals. When publishers let you examine the first volume of a book series with no obligation to buy, send you a free gift that's yours to keep even if you don't buy, and let you return any book you receive thereafter, you're more likely to trust them with your credit card number. And when an online or catalog marketer rewards frequent buyers with free shipping, gifts, and privileges, buyers are more likely to return to shop again.

Marketers who want to be around for the long haul do well to practice reciprocal altruism. Treating customers morally and ethically, giving them the benefit of the doubt, and rewarding them is good business precisely because it resonates with evolved humanity.

The first marketers who placed trust in customers admittedly took a risk. After all, just as there are greedy bats, there are greedy people. What was to keep people from returning perfectly good products and simply claiming dissatisfaction? Or from claiming not to have received a product that was in fact delivered?

Happily, experience has shown trustworthiness to be an inherent trait in the majority of humans, most of the time. It bodes well for marketing. And for humankind.

Chapter 6

What the Peppered Moth Reveals About Postcards

Before you decide not to try postcards, you might want to speak with a Peppered Moth.

In pre-industrial England, the best way for a Peppered Moth to avoid bird-food status was to inherit light coloring, perch on a tree or lichen, and blend in. But when factories and smokestacks arose, the resultant air pollution began blackening trees and killing off lichens. Against this changed background, light-colored moths became visible and, therefore, vulnerable while their newly better-hidden, dark-colored siblings flourished.

In much the same way that factories altered the English landscape, the Internet has altered the marketing landscape. Just as a changed forest gave a natural advantage to dark-colored moths, this new marketing environment seems to have given a few natural advantages to postcards.

This may require some mental adjustment for direct marketers who, like me, were raised on the sanctity of the "classic direct mail package." We conceded certain uses for postcards, but for the most part experience showed that they just couldn't measure up against an envelope loaded with sales letter, brochure, lift note, order form, and reply envelope.

But, as I wish my friend Keith Goodman of Modern Postcard hadn't reminded me, I am (well) over 50. "Envelopes don't evoke nostalgia for the rising generation that they do for us boomers," he said. "The new generation grew up hearing from friends and relatives via instant messaging, tweets, and emails. They still love getting mail, but it doesn't have to show up in an envelope anymore."

Meanwhile, the advantages of postcards in an Internet era are piling up. For instance:

Instant gratification. In an online world, people expect information and entertainment on-the-spot. This happens to be a major strength of postcards, since they require no download time. A well-executed postcard telegraphs your message faster than an envelope full of enclosures and the fastest-loading website.

Economy. Postcards let you avoid the costs of printing, addressing, matching, and inserting multiple pieces.

Natural immunities. Postcards are not subject to junk filters, opt-outs, or blacklisting. And since they arrive sans envelope, the right layout ensures that not even the most ardent mail discarder will miss your headline. Even time-management gurus who urge people to throw away direct mail unopened cannot stop their disciples from seeing the headline. (Such fiends, those time-management gurus.)

Versatility. The Internet makes it possible for postcards to succeed in arenas once deemed beyond their reach, such as fundraising and mail order selling. Postcards are proving adept at capturing interest and then sending people to websites where they can complete transactions.

Relevance. Don't be fooled by the shift of personal communications to instant messaging, tweeting, and emailing. Mail remains a powerful force. A U.S. Postal Service survey shows that "...74% of Generation X and 68% of Generation Y direct mail receivers read retail advertising mail."

After recovering from his reminding me about my age, I asked Keith for tips on making direct mail postcards work their hardest. He suggested a test that you can do yourself. After collecting your mail for a few days, spread it across the kitchen table. Note the pieces that stand out at a glance. Chances are it will be (1) the largest ones ("Bigger is better," he assured me) and (2) those with the most easily, instantly-assimilated graphics.

It's not time to abandon the tried-and-true classic direct mail package. It still works, especially for people who were raised on letters in envelopes. But to reach generations that grew up with the Internet, it may be time to take a new look at postcards.

If moths can adapt, so can we.

Chapter 7

A Woman in an Ape Suit Reveals Secrets of Online Advertising

Imagine watching a half-minute video in which two teams pass a basketball. One team wears black shirts, the other wears white. Your task is to count how many times the team members in white complete a pass.

If you are like most people, you will likely report the correct number of passes, but there's about an even chance that you will completely miss the woman in the gorilla suit. The one who walks through the game in plain sight, pauses facing the camera for a bit of chest beating, and then strides off.

By means of the gorilla challenge and other ingenious tests, cognitive psychologists Christopher Chabris and Daniel Simons have demonstrated that, try as we may, we humans simply cannot focus on more than one thing at a time. Though Chabris and Simons didn't have advertising in mind, I think the woman in the gorilla suit provides a clue as to the challenge advertisers face in an increasingly online world.

It's one thing when people visit the likes of *amazon.com*, *overstock.com*, or *walmart.com* intent on shopping. When they visit the likes of Twitter, Pinterest, or Facebook, they're not intent on shopping, but pithy remarks, shared interests, and kitten videos. Like viewers counting passes on the basketball court, they will likely see what they're looking for and not see what they're not looking for.

I hate to break it to you this way, but one of the things they're not looking for is your ad.

This is not to say that you shouldn't advertise in the social media. Many advertisers have been successful there. But since many more have not, here are some tips to bear in mind.

Target carefully. Social media will let you narrow down audiences by interest. Take advantage of that. There's no sense spending money showing up in front of the wrong people.

Be interruptive. Creative work will need to wrest attention from the content people logged on to see.

Fight kittens with kittens. Many advertisers are taking a "if you can't beam 'em, join 'em" approach. If you know that people click on kitten videos (etc.), maybe you need to find a relevant way to put kittens (etc.) in your ad. Note that word *relevant.* Gratuitous use of kittens (etc.) will not help.

The gorilla challenge and other ingenious tests are described in Chabris's and Simons's delightful book *The Invisible Gorilla and Other Ways Our Intuitions Deceive Us.* To view the above-referenced video and test your friends, visit *www. invisiblegorilla.com.*

Part Two

What Branding Is and Isn't

Chapter 8

A Direct Marketer Looks at Branding

This is embarrassing. As champions of instant, measurable results, direct response people like me are supposed to dismiss any form of advertising that doesn't make the phone ring, and ring now. Yet here I am, confessing a passion for, of all things, branding.

Branding is not typically what direct marketers like me do. Except, well, yes it is. Because all advertising, including direct response, affects the brand.

Every commercial for Time Life affects the brand. So does every J. Peterman, Levenger, and Sharper Image catalog. So does every ACLU, AARP, and AAA direct mailing. So does every Ron Popeil infomercial.

Even a message whose sole objective is to produce orders leaves an impression about the advertiser. Responsible direct marketers understand the importance of leaving the right impression, and of leaving it on purpose. They recognize that direct response advertising influences all within its reach, not just the relatively few who actually respond. A chance to leave a strong impression with the non-responding majority is a bonus marketing opportunity only a fool would waste. Moreover, smart direct marketers build their strategies upon the brand. The first half of my own agency's strategic process focuses on the brand. We grow the direct response tactics from there.

I suspect it isn't branding itself that direct marketers disdain so much as the abundant abuses that pass for it. On this point, despite other differences, responsible direct response marketers find themselves in full agreement with responsible branding agencies.

What branding isn't

Occasionally I stumble upon a company that proudly tells me they have just, at no small cost, redone their "brand." Then they lay a slogan on me, usually a lame one, along with a new or updated logo. They are so pleased with themselves and the fruits of their investment that, in an uncharacteristic show of restraint, I keep my mouth shut. This is not the time to tell them that a slogan and a logo do not a brand make.

There are as many definitions of branding as there are branding agencies and consultants. I define a brand as *the sum total of your values, as evidenced by how you deliver on those values, at every point of contact.*

Your brand is what you stand for, and what you won't stand for. It is your company's personality. It is how you will and won't do business. It is the customers you seek, and the ones you don't. It is how you treat employees, partners, vendors, and customers. It is the care that goes into your product or service. It is your overriding principles and your diligence in adhering to them. To the extent that you ride herd on your brand, it is manifest in the look and feel of your facilities, in the behavior of employees, and in all of your communications—in person, in policy, on the phone, online, in correspondence, and in advertising.

In short, a brand is the experience that you, your company and your people deliver. It is manifest in every aspect of interacting with your company.

Advertising does not create a brand. In fact, some of today's strongest brands belong to remarkably quiet advertisers. There is no Nordstrom campaign touting impeccable service and upscale décor or Starbucks campaign bragging about the aficionado behind the counter who can tell you the distinguishing characteristics of coffees from around the world. These companies have built strong brands through consistent delivery, which is the outgrowth of values backed by passion.

And, they managed to do it without help from slogans like, "Nordstrom. Great service, real marble floors."

A bit of branding history

Branding originally referred to burning one's mark on bovine rears to help ranchers distinguish among look-alike cattle.

We have the advent of the railroad to thank for the term's induction into the marketing lexicon. Railroads made mass distribution possible, which in turn made mass production viable. With mass production came knockoffs, and with knockoffs came the need for manufacturers to differentiate their products. They solved the problem by adding proprietary marks to their packaging and referring to those marks by the aptly appropriated term *brand*.

Branding worked. Consumers lined up behind preferred brands, such that it wasn't long before brands became valuable assets in and of themselves. Companies protected their brands by standardizing trademark use, prosecuting unauthorized use, and, if they were smart, refusing to put their mark on products that didn't live up to their standards.

Brand preference has evolved in two directions. The first direction centers on product *attributes*: Ruffles have ridges, Heinz ketchup is thickest. The second centers on creating an *image* to appeal to the self-concept of a market: a Levi's wearer would rather die than wear Wranglers, and vice versa.

Image marketing proved a useful solution for products with little else to distinguish them—at first. A brand could wishful-think itself an image, and attract customers who identified with that image. For instance, after an unsuccessful foray as a women's cigarette, Marlboro reintroduced itself as the cigarette for manly men. Powerful TV spots featured ruggedly handsome cowboys, puffing away as they herded cattle to music from *The Magnificent Seven*. Soon any male smoker who wanted to look manly had to smoke Marlboro, and he paid a premium price for the privilege.

Other brands without a readily apparent competitive advantage were quick to differentiate by image as well. Substance was optional. For a while and in quite a few cases, it worked. Pepsi became the cola for young people expressing individuality. Ultra Brite became the toothpaste for people with sex appeal. Jif became the peanut butter for choosy mothers.

But as brands and choices proliferated, and as consumers paid more attention to benefit-for-price-paid, brand loyalty began eroding. All but the fussiest consumers began figuring out that whether they chose Hunts, Heinz, or Del Monte tomato sauce had little effect on the outcome of their lasagna. They learned that briefs from JCPenney performed about the same as briefs from Fruit of the Loom. They noticed that cars handled equally well with radials from Goodyear or Sears.

The unthinkable was happening: despite distinctive trademarks and carefully crafted images, well-known brands were becoming parity products. Even the cowboy lost his hold, and mighty Marlboro found itself forced to commit the ultimate brand no-no: lowering the price to compete.

Pseudo branding

Justifiably panicked, marketers today have reacted by becoming increasingly evangelical about the need to build and maintain powerful brands. That's a good idea. It becomes a bad idea only when they try to build a brand by advertising a wishfully thought-up, substance-less image.

Times have changed. Linking your brand to a cowboy is no longer enough. After 50 years of shallow images and incessant clutter, consumers are no longer so easily charmed to the cash register. Today, the practice of claiming to be unique without bothering to change anything but your advertising is not branding, but *pseudo branding*.

More and more companies, stuck in the past, fall prey to pseudo branding. A company runs a campaign telling you they're different in the way they think, hire, and behave. But upon visiting their place of business, you find a bank, grocery store, insurance company, or department store that looks, feels, and acts like any other. This is not branding. It is letting your customer down.

Or, they come up with a slogan that makes the board of directors puff their chests but leaves the market unmoved. This is not branding. It is talking to yourself.

Today's consumers demand more than pretension. They demand substance. At the cash register, they reward those who deliver it.

Five Tests of Brand Strength

If you and I were playing a friendly game of Word Association and I happened to toss out "brand enthusiast," I bet that "direct marketer" wouldn't be the first thing you'd toss back. "Brand shmand," many a direct marketer is wont to say. "Does it sell or not?"

Point taken, but let's not throw out the brand with the bath water. A strong brand makes any direct marketer's job easier. Take, for example, Omaha Steaks. They charge a small fortune plus shipping fees for a frozen, four-ounce, uncooked filet mignon. Call me cynical, but I doubt that anyone would pay that price for an identical filet mignon at Sizzler if they served one.

Do you have a strong brand? Below are five, revealing tests of brand strength that we use at the RESPONSE Agency. But first, a word on what branding *isn't*. It's important not to mistake a logo, graphic look, or tagline for a brand. Logos et al serve only to identify which products and services are *Yours*. You give the concept of *Yours* equity through consistent delivery. The brand gives the logo meaning, not the other way around. A solid brand is the by-product of doing things right.

On to the five tests:

1. *The Masked Logo Test:* If you hid your logo, would customers be able to tell your product or service from that of the competition by the experience you create for them? A yes indicates a strong brand. A no indicates you're not as different as you think.

2. *The Fickle Customer Test:* Would your customers readily jilt you for a lower-priced look-alike? A no indicates a strong brand. A yes indicates that, to your customers, you're just another commodity.

3. *The Oh Come On Test:* Do people believe your claims, or pass them off as empty boasts? A yes indicates a strong brand. A no indicates you're pretty good at kidding yourself, and possibly at failing to notice as your customers roll their eyes and say, "Oh come on."

4. *The Value Statement Transplant Test:* About those values immortalized on your wall—could your competitors lay equal claim to them? A no indicates a strong brand. A yes indicates your value statement may be an exercise in spewing the usual hot air.

5. *The Do Your Employees Get It Test:* Can you tell from your employees' behavior that they embrace the values that you think you stand for? A yes indicates a strong brand. A no indicates that you may have communicating and training to do, policies to revise, systems to re-design, or any combination of the above.

You can have a strong brand.

Sometimes I summarize the five tests this way, with apologies to those who'd rather I not play around with the Epistle of James: "Show me your brand without your works, and I will show you my brand by my works. O foolish man, a brand without works is dead."

To be fair, no law says you absolutely must build a brand that will endure for centuries. Marketing history brims with flash in-the-pan campaigns that sold oodles with little regard to the brand: Ginsu Knife, the Abdomenizer, the Smokeless Ash Tray, Pet Rock, and Snuggie. If you want to capitalize on a momentarily open window, there is no shame in going for it.

But marketers who want to prosper for the long haul need staying power. As windows close, fads pass, and knockoffs arise, the foundation of staying power is laid in the brand.

Chances are the makings of a strong brand already exist within your company, or within the minds of its leadership. The trick is to uncover your brand, develop it, live it, and vigilantly ensure its delivery at every point of contact.

This will require, among other things, leadership. Posters in the break room and ads that say "customers come first" fall flat when the CEO plays hermit. Branding begins at the top. Values trickle down, never up.

If you need help discovering and delivering on your brand promise, there are many fine firms, including ad agencies, who can help. But should someone try to sell you a cute slogan and a cool logo as your new brand, hold on to your wallet and run away.

With your brand in place, your ad agency can get to work. Whether you give them objectives for building brand awareness, selling products or both, they will be able to build their work on a solid foundation.

Chapter 9

Brandbabble

Call me a cynic, but I think it's no coincidence that just about every ad agency's definition of "brand" happens to align with that agency's area of strength.

Designers like to equate a brand with what the rest of us call "corporate identity," that is, a consistent visual presentation. Creative directors often equate it with so-called "breakthrough" creative work. Researchers often equate it with a representative sample's ability to regurgitate a product name unassisted. Wordsmiths often equate it with a would-be catchy tagline, usually an empty or weak one, like the newspaper in my home state of Utah that came up with no better than "News for your world."

All of the above is naught but brandbabble.

No brand emerges from a look, memorability, or a tagline. It's the other way around. If you first have a brand, then from it will emerge a look, memorability, and, if you must have one, perhaps a tagline.

Work on your logo, tagline, and other noisemaking last. Start by defining your values. Then make sure you deliver on them—online, on the phone, in the store, and face-to-face with customers, vendors, and employees. Do that, and your brand will speak for itself.

Chapter 10

Direct Marketers Should Embrace Branding

I f you rank among direct marketers who excel at pronouncing "branding" with a sneer, it's time to relent. Though immediate sales once reigned while branding was fluff, like it or not, today legitimate branding has become a big part of the business you're in.

For a number of good reasons, even the most ardent, bottom-line driven direct marketers care about branding these days. For one thing, markets respond to strong brands. If you don't believe me, try getting a consumer to pay a Sharper Image price for an air purifier from Walmart. For another, though brand perception is not its primary calling, direct marketing leaves an impression among far more people than those who respond. While we throw wild parties to commemorate a four percent response, non respondents—the 96 percent—also receive an impression about the brand. And, for yet another, branding is *the* hot marketing topic these days. If you don't know anything about it, sooner or later, you're going to look dumb. Or, worse, capture short-term sales at the expense of the long term.

To be fair, abuses in the name of branding deserve a sneer. Every day, one more branding charlatan convinces yet another trusting client that a brand consists of a cool logo and a lame slogan. Or a company tries to convey a brand that doesn't reflect practice, like the store that promises you a great shopping experience, even though everyone knows the aisles are cluttered, the lighting is insufficient, and the minimum wage clerk would rather prolong a personal call than notice you.

But branding—real, bona fide branding—is powerful stuff. It's what lets you walk into Nordstrom expecting first-rate quality and service, and into Kohl's pretty much braced to fend for yourself. It's what tells you that you can count on getting the same Big Mac from any McDonald's anywhere in the U.S. It's what makes a teenager eschew or swear by a particular brand of jeans.

That kind of brand strength arises from a company's consistent values and behavior. Advertising and direct marketing, powerless to create it, can only reflect it.

But the wrong advertising and direct marketing can weaken a brand. That presents an interesting problem. As a direct marketer, you're hired to bring in a profitable, measurable response, not to build the brand. But if you don't recognize the impact your work has on the brand, and, perhaps more important, that the brand should have on your work, you're being naive, and you will lose sales in the long run.

Dyed-in-the-wool DM companies understand this, and have built strong brands. Consider Geico, Levenger, Brookstone, and, yes, Ron Popeil. Each brand has its distinct practices, product lines, customer profiles, and look and feel. The moment Levenger starts acting like Ron Popeil, they will lose loyal customers. And vice versa.

My advice to direct marketing experts is that they also become branding experts. Otherwise, they will soon find themselves laughed out of marketing meetings at the strategic level. Worse, they may sell now, but miss an opportunity to help position a company for success over the long haul.

Chapter 11

Direct Response or Branding: Which Way Should You Go?

Whenever I'm asked to sum up the differences between traditional and direct response advertising, I oversimplify it this way:

Traditional advertising takes an *indirect* approach. It seeks to create positive awareness of a product in the backs of minds so that, eventually, your target market will attribute to your brand a certain *je ne sais quoi* and reach for it instead of a competing brand. Campaigns of this kind have had their share of overnight successes—Volkswagen's "think small," Avis's "we try harder," Benson & Hedges's "oh the disadvantages"—but, more often, an awareness campaign needs years to take hold. Viewers weren't too sure about Wendy's Dave Thomas at first, but embraced him over time.

Which means that traditional brand advertising is the kind of advertising you may need to run for a few years before you know whether or not you want to fire your ad agency. Direct response advertising agencies have improved on that. We know how to get fired in about 60 days.

The distinguishing characteristic of *direct response advertising* is the fact that it asks the target market to respond *directly* and *immediately* to the advertiser. Usually this means asking the market to visit a web site, reply to an email, place a phone call, mail a card, or walk into a place of business.

It follows that direct response advertising is eminently measurable. Direct marketers are not interested in how many people remember an ad or report feeling more inclined to buy their client's product after seeing it. People respond or they don't. Awareness happens, but it happens as a by-product.

Which is both good and bad. It's good for clients, for they know what they're getting in return for their advertising dollar. It's only good for direct response agencies when their work performs. When it doesn't, there's no place to hide.

There is room—in fact, need—in the world for both kinds of advertising. McDonald's would be foolish to abandon image-building ads. So would Coca-Cola. On the other hand, Geico Insurance would be equally foolish to give up their charming "call now for a free quote" spots to settle on increasing the awareness of geckos.

Most agencies that are good at one usually aren't at the other, though both tend indignantly to argue the point. The strategic thinking and skill set needed for an awareness campaign are entirely different from those needed for a response campaign. Awareness advertising needs to break through clutter, command attention, and implant itself in as many memories as possible. Direct response advertising (DR) must also break through clutter, but its goal is not so much to be remembered as to be acted upon without delay.

So it is that differing tactics emerge. Awareness TV spots air when the greatest number of targeted viewers are likely to be watching. DR spots air when viewers are fewer in number, but are more likely to leave the tube to make the suggested phone call or visit the suggested website. Awareness print ads tend to be short and punchy. DR ads tend to be longer in order to give readers enough information to make a buying decision. Awareness approaches can afford to tease and entertain. DR approaches must get quickly to the point.

It's not unusual for awareness agencies to dismiss DR agencies as champions of the straightforward and boring, and for DR agencies to accuse awareness agencies of sacrificing effectiveness on the altar of artistic fulfillment. Direct marketers will blurt out, "If it doesn't sell, it isn't creative." Awareness advertisers hurl back, "If it isn't creative, it won't sell."

Amid the zeal of each to establish the other as the Antichrist of advertising, both camps could benefit from and possibly get along with one another better with a little perspective. To wit:

• Not all highly creative ads are intrinsically irresponsible.

• Not all response-oriented ads are fated to bore.

• If any ad campaign fails to meet its objectives, its creative quality or lack thereof is moot.

• Not all ad campaigns have hard sales objectives. Sometimes the objective is to change an advertiser's image, as IBM does with upbeat ads to shed their stodgy aura. (Not that it always works. Witness Oldsmobile.) Sometimes the objective is to effect behavior change, as with antismoking campaigns. Sometimes the objective is to decrease the likelihood of waking up one day to find headquarters surrounded by protesters, as oil companies hope to do with ads showing pristine land under which you'd never suspect reposes a pipeline.

• On the other hand, sometimes the sole advertising objective really is to make cash registers ring without regard for the long-term impression the ad leaves behind.

• More often, objectives call for some balance, which is why an increasing number of direct marketing campaigns are as attractive and charming as they are productive and accountable.

• Certain creative approaches work well for some objectives, and poorly for others. If you want to convince people that your wrench is more reliable than others, you're going to need some straightforward sales talk about what it's made from, how many pounds of torque it can take, how easy it is to grip, and more. Some might call the resultant ad long and boring, but a mechanic in need of a serious wrench will gobble up every word. On the other hand, if you want to convince people that you have the hottest nightclub in town, chances are that a glitzy, fast-paced TV spot with hard-driving music will serve you better than a detailed description of the materials that went into the dance floor.

You may have noticed something that the above points have in common. They underscore the importance of establishing clear advertising objectives long before you mull creative approaches. Objectives are the standard by which you should evaluate proposed concepts, and by which you should measure a campaign's success.

If you think the importance of establishing objectives should be obvious, I'd have to agree: It should be. But you'd be surprised at how often advertisers overlook establishing objectives to guide their work and, later, overlook returning to objectives to evaluate it. More than one company has restricted its ad agency to image-enhancing campaigns and, when sales didn't promptly rise, threatened to stop advertising altogether. You don't paint a house with the objective of making it sell faster only to declare new paint a failure for not increasing the house's selling price.

If you're wondering whether your company should go with traditional or direct response advertising, review your objectives. If awareness, recognition and public favor are essential parts of your marketing plan, consider awareness advertising. If your goals include quantifiable leads, inquiries, sales, or dialog with customers and prospects, you should take a look at direct response. If your objectives fall in both areas, you may benefit from a little of both.

Chapter 12

The Power of Not Pleasing Everyone

In a fable attributed to Aesop, onlookers criticize a man and his son for walking alongside a perfectly ride-worthy donkey. If one of them rides, onlookers criticize him for making the other walk. When both ride, onlookers accuse them of animal cruelty. At length, they resolve to carry the donkey. This incites ridicule and, worse, an accident in which the animal falls to its death. The moral: Try to please all and you will please none.

Aesop could have been talking about brands.

Successful brands know who their customers are and seek to please them. Snickers positions itself as a satisfying snack for people who want to justify a candy bar between meals, BMW for luxury aficionados who want to show the world that they can afford a BMW, and Starbucks for the would-be coffee connoisseur.

But some marketers experience angst upon realizing that knowing who your customer *is* inevitably means knowing who your customer *isn't*, and that attempting to appeal to both inevitably means compromising your appeal to either.

The need to focus a brand's appeal is more than an inescapable concession to the way things are. It is strategically sound. Imagine the effect on the brand if Snickers began targeting dieters, BMW introduced a low-price model, or Starbucks opened a diner. Any such attempt would at once fall flat and weaken the brand's credibility with its established market.

If you're loath to commit to not being all things to all people, you're not alone. Brands you know have learned the hard way. When IBM responded to cooler, hipper Apple Computer by trying to appear cool and hip in its own right, Apple's devotees weren't impressed, and IBM's established customers who weren't too sure they recognized the maker of their old, reliable products anymore. When Kmart introduced celebrity-endorsed clothing straight from the pages of fashion magazines, it swayed no new upscale shoppers, and its loyal, budget-minded customers feared abandonment. And when Gerber tried to sell the likes of pureed creamed beef to single adults in relabeled baby food jars (I didn't make that up), their core and desired markets both responded with a resounding "Ugh."

If you want to attract new markets, there are better ways. One approach is to find new uses for your product. Perhaps your juice isn't just for breakfast anymore. Maybe your baking soda can deodorize refrigerators and cat boxes. Maybe your cooking spray can be used to keep grass clippings from sticking to the underside of a lawn mower.

Or, you might introduce a new brand. You can probably name a certain automobile manufacturer with distinct high, middle, and low end brands (hint: Toyota), a clothing marketer with three differently branded retail chains (hint: Gap, Inc.), and a cola company with an array of separately branded non-cola drinks (hint: the Coca-Cola Company). The identity of the parent companies is no secret—in fact, the parentage lends credibility—but each brand remains distinct so as to appeal to its core market without compromise.

It takes courage to stick to the "who is and is not our customer" part of a brand. But it's wiser and less risky to focus on being just-right for the few than to risk being not-quite-right for the many.

Take it from Aesop. You can't please everyone. If you try, you may end up falling flat on your, um, donkey.

Part Three

Unpardonable Copywriting Sins

Chapter 13

Copy Cop-Outs

10 Signs of a Lazy Copywriter

This chapter was born one morning as I shouted at the car radio on my way to work. I had to make do with shouting at the radio because the lazy copywriter who'd resorted to "people who care" was nowhere near for me to throttle.

Maybe I'm different. Maybe the rest of world says, "Holy smokes! If that company has people who care, I'm giving them my business from now on." But to me, it's a Copy Cop-Out. A platitude masquerading as a claim. A hallmark of writers too lazy to dig out and present a viable benefit.

Copy Cop-Outs abound. Here are ten that I enjoy hating the most:

1. *"People who care."* Until the competition starts bragging about having people who *don't* care, "people who care" won't set you apart. Besides, I don't believe you. I mean, have you visited one of your stores lately?

2. *"Only the finest ingredients."* Yeah, like your chef visits the market each morning to handpick the plumpest tomatoes. But if your chef *does*, put THAT in your ad.

3. *"Our people are trained professionals."* Society tends to reserve the word "professional" for the likes of doctors and lawyers. Don't try convincing me that the teen in greasy over-

alls working the lube pit is a professional. If you gave the teen exhaustive training and refused to turn him or her loose on my car without passing a rigorous exam, put THAT in your ad.

4. *"All your needs."* Compare "Over 100,000 hard-to-find foreign car parts in stock" and "For all your foreign car part needs." Which do you think is stronger?

5. *"A tradition of…"* If you believe tradition is a compelling copy point, consider the ongoing decline in holiday fruitcake sales.

6. *"We were first."* Being *first* in the consumer mind is strong. *Whining about being first* is pathetic. Root beer and orange soda were around long before Doc Pemberton invented Coca-Cola. I am willing to bet that that bit of trivia will not move anyone who loves Coke to switch.

7. *"Friendly service."* Everybody says that. We don't believe them any more than we believe you.

8. *"Serving you since…"* If people cared how long who has been serving whom, Walmart wouldn't have overtaken Sears.

9. *"Proud to be…"* Bully for you, but I don't care what you're proud of. I want to know what you'll do for me.

10. *"Your partner."* A partner invests and shares risk. You, by contrast, have something to sell me. Quit wasting your breath and my time with partner talk and give me some good reasons to buy.

Chapter 14

More Copy Cop-Outs

Doing a live commercial on the radio can't be easy. How radio personalities manage to sound sincere while extolling another tire shop, electrolysis center, or restaurant is beyond me. Imagine the cynical remarks your favorite hosts must vent when they're off the air.

Let the record to show that I am not criticizing radio hosts. I don't wish to be unkind. More important, I don't want to make them mad, especially at me, especially when they're on the air.

But I will politely suggest that radio hosts retire the phrase "that everyone's talking about." No, everyone is *not* talking about the advertised product. I have personally witnessed moments when everyone was actually talking about something else. "The new enema service that everyone's talking about" is meaningless, a platitude masquerading as a claim, a phrase that consumes time but adds nothing.

In short, it's a Copy Cop-Out.

Copy Cop-Outs rear their ugly heads in puns, too. Why is it that a line sure to draw groans in a social setting draws industry accolades when you stick it in an ad?

Another means of copping out is to make the product a prop in an entertaining scenario about something else. All this shows is that you find the product too boring to command attention with its own benefits.

Here's a good way to avoid a Copy Cop-Out: Never lead with the product name. If the first word of your first line is the name of the product, you have missed a chance to lead with something that matters to your customer.

The ever popular smart-aleck tone can be a Copy Cop-Out. Not everything has to be funny. Mind you, I am an incurable, compulsive smart-aleck. I wisecrack throughout this book and throughout my life. Still, even I acknowledge that there are times to hold back.

Once I chanced upon a smart-alecky, pun-laden ad *for a cemetery*. Under a photo of a grave-studded hill overlooking the city, the headline joked about "exclusive view lots." Now, the cemetery market comprises people approaching their own death, people whose loved one is approaching death, or people trying to hold themselves together because a loved one's death just took them unawares and unprepared. None of these is the right time to yuck it up. As for me, only moments before seeing the ad, I had come upon the obituary of a close friend who, I learned, had taken his own life. Not even this smart aleck was in the mood for joking about view lots. A warm and caring tone may be a cliché for the funeral industry, but it's a cliché for a reason.

Looking for a cure for the common Copy Cop-Out? I suggest working a little harder.

Chapter 15

Still More Copy Cop-Outs

Laziness begets writers. At least it did in my case. One of the reasons I write is so I can avoid doing real work.

But I try to avoid letting laziness show in my writing. Perhaps that explains my ongoing tirade against Copy Cop-Outs, my term for meaningless phrases at the expense of substance. Here is a new offering of pet-peeve Copy Cop-Outs. The more writers learn to avoid them, the greater the odds are that they will write ads that actually say something.

"Simply the best." Trust me on this: no one will read that and say, "That's good enough for me!" If you really think you're the best, try *showing* instead of *telling*. Don't just say "Simply the best paint job." Say "We apply three coats of paint where others apply just one." Don't settle for saying "Simply the strongest." Say "We use steel where others use plastic." Don't say "Simply the freshest." Say "We make our hollandaise sauce to order from scratch, never from a mix."

"Best on the planet." This is no more convincing than its equally meaningless, equally impotent predecessor, "best in the world." Planet or world, no one believes you. You didn't conduct an exhaustive, planet-wide search to ensure the inferiority of all competing products. Pinned down, all you could do is whine, *"Wellllll ... I* think it's the best ... and so do my parents, spouse, kids, and at least one cousin twice removed ..."

Superlatives in general. Lest my diatribes against phrases like "simply the best" and "best on the planet" make you think that I am waging a war against superlatives, permit me to set the record straight: I am. The movie *Two Weeks Notice* neatly exposes the problem. When Sandra Bullock's character says, "I think you're the most selfish human being on the planet," Hugh Grant's character replies, "Well that's just silly. Have you met everybody on the planet?"

"Our name says it all." Really? Then run ads with your name and nothing else.

"That's right!" / *"You heard right!"* Do you really think the special deal in your radio spot will make listeners reel and wonder if they heard right?

"Combined experience." Let's do some math. Twenty-five years of combined experience divided by 50 employees works out to an average of six months of experience per employee. I'm not impressed.

"At a price you're going to love." Then put the price in the ad. When you tell people they're going to love the price but you don't tell them what the price is, you call attention to the fact that you're withholding it, and they don't believe you.

"If you find a lower price, we'll meet or beat it." Some promise. You'll only have to make good in the rare instance of an obsessive customer with sufficient time to compare and return with proof of a better deal. And if at that point all you do is meet the price—you said "meet *or* beat," but I have hunch which one it will be—your customer could have saved time

and trouble by going to your lower-priced competitor in the first place.

"Ad agency trying to have an idea." This offense turns up often in radio spots. The setting is a creative brainstorming session. A voice says, "We could say that we have the best service." A second voice adds, "Or, we could say that we guarantee our work," and so on until you have covered every "could say" imaginable. It makes me want to cry out, "Pick one and say it, or shut up." On second thought, just shut up.

"Slice of production life." In another abuse that frequents the radio waves, the voice talent stops halfway through reading the copy to say, "This sounds too good to be true. Are you sure this script is right?" Someone in the control booth assures the talent that, yes, the script is right and adds a few more benefits while the talent responds with *oohs, ahs,* and *mm-hmmms.* Finally, we hear footsteps running away. The producer yells, "Where are you going? We haven't finished the commercial." The talent's distant voice yells back something about having to get to the store to take advantage of this great deal. I believe we are expected to chuckle.

"Can't describe it." Here the writer, after telling us that the product's goodness defies description, resorts to a would-be humorous analogy to dramatize the product's indescribability. Something along the line of, "It's like trying to explain compromise to Congress." Translation: "I may not be able to come up with a convincing strategy, but at least I can't come up with a good one-liner, either."

"We're not like that." Service industries often resort to this one. Rather than dramatize a company's positive attributes, they dramatize the competition's negative attributes, usually with a touch of what they suppose to be humor. Then they sum up, "We're not like that." In other words, they tell us what they're *not* (as bad as the other guys) while at the same time inadvertently demonstrating something else they're *not* (funny). They would do better to tell us what they *are*.

Chapter 16

No Mercy for Any Who Pen "For All Your Needs"

If you write "for all your needs," you deserve no mercy in this life or any alleged life to come. And don't think that plopping a modifier in front of "needs" will save you. "For all your hair care needs" is no better.

It's your job is to identify needs and show how a product fills them. "For all your needs" attempts to shove that job onto customers. They won't accept the assignment, so it's not a terribly effective line.

Imagine the consumer who exclaims, "It says right here that Honest Mikey's Mortgage & Deli is the place for all my home loan needs. Surely this is the mortgage banker for me!" Something like "step-by-step, easy-to-understand guidance for the first-time home buyer," "approvals in 24 hours," or "pay off your loan sooner and save tens of thousands of dollars in interest" might persuade a bit more.

Dessert menus do not say, "For all your sweet tooth needs." Mace ads do not say, "For all your mugger avoidance needs." Carpet stores do not advertise, "For all your floor-covering needs."

Oh, wait. Carpet stores often do, and they shouldn't.

Chapter 17

A Study on the Selling Power of Slogans

I cringed this morning when I read an article purporting to share advice on launching a successful business. The author claimed that after deciding upon a product or service, the next step was to come up with a "catchy slogan." The article appeared in a national magazine. Heaven only knows how many more lame slogans you and I will have to endure as a result.

To be fair, there are good slogans. It's hard to argue with a catchy line that also happens to be descriptive, believable and persuasive. There was power in FedEx's "When it absolutely positively has to be there overnight," charm in the double-negative "Everybody doesn't like something, but nobody doesn't like Sara Lee," and, going back a few years, credibility in the old Timex line, "Takes a licking and keeps on ticking."

But needless, lame slogans abound in greater number than needful, strong ones, thanks to insecure marketers who fear a brand isn't a brand unless they dollop it with a flatulent parting boast. Often they add a TM or ®,* putting the world on notice that they and only they have exclusive rights to the likes of "Proudly serving you" (lest we suspect them of embarrassedly serving us), "We're the professionals" (setting them apart from those who say "We're the hacks"), "We care" (in case you mistook a clerk's ignoring you for not caring), or "A tradition of excellence" (differentiates from those who stake their reputation on a tradition of mediocrity).

Not to be overlooked are myriad "people" slogans, like "Our people make the difference." Sticking "people" in your slogan neither humanizes nor endears you. It will not set your business apart until your competitors start using slogans like "Our feral cats make the difference," "Proudly hiring the dregs of society," or "Nincompoops serving nincompoops for over 50 years."

Bad slogans are not the exclusive domain of amateurs. One of the reasons small companies feel they need to come up with a lame slogan is that so many large ones do.

The Mini Study

I wanted to know if slogans sell anything. To find out, I conducted a mini-study. I grabbed a few random issues of *Reader's Digest*, which carries an abundance of branding and direct response ads alike. I cut out and separated the branding and response ads into two piles. Then I counted how many ads in each pile had and didn't have a slogan.

Branding agencies tend to rely on inferential methods such as recall, recognition, and awareness to measure the effectiveness of their work. Direct response agencies rely on cold, hard sales. I reasoned, therefore, that it's fair to assume that while brand marketers may know if slogans move products, direct response marketers must surely know.

Would you care to guess the percentage of direct response ads versus branding ads in my study that had a slogan?

Every branding ad had at least one slogan. Some had two. One had three, which, I suppose, didn't say much for the advertiser's confidence in the first two. As for the direct response ads, *none had slogans.*

It appears that slogans appeal more to advertisers who are less likely to know their value than to advertisers who are more likely to know.

If that doesn't tell you something about the overall value of slogans, you're stubborn.

If you cannot restrain yourself from cooking up a slogan, perhaps there is no harm in it. But at least avoid the kind of self-indulgent drivel that impresses no one but the Board of Directors and their closest relatives. Devise a line that's relevant, credible, and compelling *from the market's point of view.*

Or, nix the slogan and invest your effort where it will actually do some good. Say, on the rest of the ad.

---

*What's the difference? The TM and the ® both say "hands off, this is mine" and can hold up in court. The TM denotes a common law claim that anyone can use. To use the ®, you must go through a registration process. In the U.S., neither symbol establishes that you own the mark. You establish ownership by being the first to *use* the mark *across states lines*. I should add that I am not an attorney, and that the foregoing is not intended to provide legal advice. In other words, if what I have written here gets you in trouble, sue somebody else.

Chapter 18

Hot Air Doth Not Credible Advertising Make

I just found this gem on a bank's home page: "To us, [our city] is not a 'market' ... While some banks are looking to make a profit, we want to make a difference, one person at a time."

You might ask how anyone could write such palpably self-serving, disingenuous drivel. Were it true that management didn't give priority to profit-making, shareholders would call for their heads. But do not underrate the power of palpably self-serving, disingenuous drivel. It can beguile a writer and gratify the stuffed shirts who approve it while remaining blissfully oblivious to the fact that customers will ignore the line or roll their eyes and say, "Oh come on."

Palpably self-serving, disingenuous drivel is not harmless. It wastes your budget on words that accomplish nothing, insults your target market's intelligence, and strips the rest of your message of credibility. When that happens, you're no longer marketing. You're making easily tuned-out noise.

To protect against the beguilement of self-serving drivel, I highly recommend applying the Oh Come On Test. It consists of three steps: 1) Slip into a pair of your market's shoes. 2) Be honest with yourself. 3) See if what you wrote strikes a chord or makes you roll your eyes and say "Oh come on." If it's the latter, that's what the delete key is for.

Step 2, the part about self-honesty, is the hardest one. Like parents who have homely children but find them beautiful, which is a good thing, advertisers are loath to take a dispassionate look at their own beloved creations, which is not.

Sometimes advertising makes claims that are technically true but, come on, admit it, they're contrived to mislead. "Second to none" may seem to say "best," but what it really says is "equal to the competition." Advertisers can get away with "clinically proven" no matter how poorly controlled and hopelessly biased their so-called "clinical trial" was. In large type, Purina's Waggin' Train dog treats package claims "100% REAL!" I challenge you to name a tangible product that isn't.

Some advertisers simply make empty claims because they like the sound of them. They'll say "we put customers first" without shopping their own stores, stepping up training, or better screening employees. I recall an uncomfortable conversation with a client who really believed that "To us you're family" was not just true but convincing. Depending on your family, I pointed out, the thought could terrify.

Generous application of the Oh Come On Test early and often can help rid your marketing of such embarrassments and leave room for substantive copy points in their place.

We routinely apply the Oh Come On Test to our own work at the RESPONSE Agency. It has saved us more than once. For a hearing aid that filters out unwanted background noise, one of our writers came up with copy that claimed, "You may be the envy of people with so-called 'normal' hearing." Fortunately, we have a quality control guy. He spotted and pruned the line before the ad went to the client for approval. "It flunks the Oh Come On Test," he said.

Dare I admit? I am the one who penned the offending line. No one is immune.

Chapter 19

We Doesn't Write Letters

When you send out a sales letter or email, you're not fooling anyone. Readers know it's an ad in letter form. But if you write it properly, it will feel personal. Do that, and many readers will suspend their disbelief long enough to hear you out.

It's important not to break the spell. Here are some common spell-breaking mistakes to avoid:

1. **"We."** *We* doesn't write letters. *I* does. Use the first person singular when referring to yourself: "I am writing you because," "I thought you might be interested in," "I urge you to consider." Do NOT say, "We are writing you because," "We thought you might be interested in," or "We urge you to consider."

2. **Not addressing the reader as "you."** If *I* writes the letter, then it follows that *you* reads it. Address the reader as "you," not "the reader" or "the customer."

3. **No greeting.** "Dear ..." says "this is a letter." Use the customer's name when possible and when it's worth the expense. When it isn't, don't be afraid of "Dear Friend," "Dear Concerned Citizen," "Dear Neighbor," or whatever. I won't say they're not corny. I'll only say that they work better than your intuition tells you.

4. **Opening with what you're proud of.** A letter that opens with "For over 50 years, we at Monoflarb Corporation

have been proud to ..." will only lose readers. The opening line's job is to make the reader want to go to the next line. No one cares what you're proud of, much less how long you've been proud of it.

5. No signature. Reproduce a hand signature, or what looks like one, at the bottom, over your printed name. If your signature is illegible, or if you don't want your real signature in circulation, create a substitute. My real signature is a scribble, but I have a legible version for letters and greeting cards. Black ink or toner is OK, but blue is best. Avoid red.

6. More than one signature. Two or more signatures say "we." You may recall that *we* doesn't write letters.

7. No P.S. Readers usually look at the signature first. While their eyes are in the vicinity, they will likely read a P.S. before returning to the top of the page. That makes the P.S. a great place to hook interest.

8. Scary job title. A good title can give you credibility, but titles like "Director of Marketing," "Sales Manager," and "Customer Relations" put readers on their guard. If you're the VP of Sales and Marketing, just put "Vice President." If you're not a VP, come up with something suitably impressive but vague, like "Project Manager."

9. Writing it yourself. Due respect, but if you write like most clients I've known, or even most ad writers, it would probably be worth your money to hire a specialist. There's a reason people like me make a living writing sales letters.

Chapter 20

Language Evolves. Live With It.

Clinging to a word's original meaning despite its having evolved a new one is known as the Genetic Fallacy. Regardless of your friendly neighborhood pedant's whines, a word's definition and use are determined by how large numbers of real people define and use it. Nor do I care what your outdated dictionary says. Dictionaries do not lead but follow the language.

Not long ago, columnist Joel Hilton lamented that the "... only time we should use the word 'viral' is when we immediately follow it with the word 'infection." Nonsense. *Viral* as used in the context of social media is correct precisely because vast numbers of people understand, accept, and use it that way.

Don't get me wrong. It still matters whether you use *affect* or *effect, discrete* or *discreet, compliment* or *complement,* and *their* or *there* or *they're.* But there is no longer any shame in using *over* in place of *more than, anxious* in place of *eager,* and *hopefully* in place of the decidedly snobbish *it is to be hoped.*

When enough people misuse a word or assign it a new meaning, the new use becomes correct. That is how language works. Witness what *gay* meant not long ago and what it commonly means today. *Decimate* offers another example. And consider that today it's acceptable to say *It's me*. One utters the technically correct *It is I* at the risk of sounding weird.

There is a fine line between holding to correct use and being an immovable grouch who denies the dynamic nature of language. I shudder at the thought—and here I admit to a bit of the entrenched pedant—but *literally* may be on its way to meaning *figuratively but emphatically* ... *infer* to meaning *imply* ... *comprised* to meaning *composed* ... and, worst of all, *penultimate* to meaning *ultimater than ultimate*.

Confusion and outrage naturally erupt during any transition. If *criteria* is destined to become acceptable as a singular as well as a plural, my advice is to sit back, relax and enjoy the *phenomena*.

But let's not be absurd. If you out-and-out misuse a word, you cannot hide behind the dynamic nature of language. I had a college roommate who insisted that *transvestite* meant *transsexual*. When I settled the matter with an appeal to the dictionary and a look at the root *vest*, he could not bring himself to concede. "Fine," he said, "but that's changing."

Part Four

Strategy Matters

Chapter 21

12 Steps to Lousy Marketing

You don't hear much about the Fourth Law of Thermodynamics. It states that when a server says "This plate is hot," an invisible force compels the customer to touch the plate. The compulsion grows as the cube of the temperature of the plate.

Given a choice between heeding a voice of experience and sabotaging ourselves, many people do not just opt but positively execute a mad dash for the latter. This can be as true of marketers as it is of other humanlike creatures. So, for those bent on their own destruction, I offer the following personally witnessed, sure-fire shortcuts. I should add that narrowing them down to twelve wasn't easy.

Sabotage Tip 1: Don't set meaningful objectives. You're much safer stating that your goal is to "get your name out there." Or, to advertise because the competition does. That way, even if sales tank, you can sit back and say, "I did my job."

Sabotage Tip 2: Paint your target around the dart after it has stuck in the wall. Setting hard objectives up front can be terribly inconvenient if you happen not to meet them. Why not wait until campaign results are in and then write your objectives to match?

Sabotage Tip 3: Authorize as many people as possible to revise or outright veto all creative work. This will ensure that creative people avoid trying to connect with the market in favor of creating what is sure to fly internally.

Sabotage Tip 4: It's about what YOU want. There's no telling how any customers Starbucks lost before CEO Howard Schultz allowed baristas to make lattes with skim milk. Schultz resisted because he wanted Starbucks to make lattes with whole milk, the way Italian baristas made them. Why should customers have a say in how they want their coffee?

Sabotage Tip 5: Misuse research. Never mind that focus groups, mall intercepts, interviews, and telephone and online surveys are not predictive. They're easy and you can make them yield the results you're hoping for.

Sabotage Tip 6: Don't listen to your salespeople. The only thing your salespeople do is interact face-to-face with your customers every day and sell them your products. What could they possibly know about marketing?

Sabotage Tip 7: If it's wild and creative, go with it. If you have a killer concept that's destined to take top honors at the next awards show, it would be a sin not to back it with your budget. It deserves to be shared, if only for art's sake.

Sabotage Tip 8: Don't test. If Nature had intended for us to conduct valid, predictive tests, we wouldn't have hips to shoot from.

Sabotage Tip 9: Don't trust your agency. They may have experts on staff, but you can still hobble them by overruling their expertise with your intuition. You can also focus on minutiae. For instance, make the art director change a border from black to dark blue and reduce a photo to 98 percent of its original size.

Sabotage Tip 10: Trust your agency. Not trusting experts is self-sabotage, but so is trusting non-experts. Many agencies claim every marketing discipline under the sun as a core competency, whether or not they have or even understand it. This is no time for due diligence. Just hand them the checkbook.

Sabotage Tip 11: A new slogan solves everything. Imagine a person who is fast losing friends. Surely there is no better way to regain popularity than to don a T-shirt that says, "The One Everybody Likes."

Sabotage Tip 12: Disdain proven techniques that you don't like. Facts hamper creativity.

There are many more ways to sabotage marketing, but this should give you a good start. If you fail to implement these recommendations, don't come whining to me if your marketing succeeds.

Chapter 22

The Wacky World of the Decoy Offer

The international magazine *The Economist* offered three subscription options. Option A: For a modest price, you could have the online edition. Option B: For about twice as much, you could have the printed edition instead. Option C: For the same price as the printed edition alone, you could have both the printed and online edition.

If you think that no fool would choose Option B, you will be pleased to know that no fool was likely to. Option B pulled its weight by acting as what behavioral economists call a *decoy offer*. Rather than attempt to garner sales of its own, its job was to draw attention away from the less-costly Option A by virtue of its stark contrast in value to Option C. In effect, B showed that C was a heckuva deal not to be missed.

In tests omitting Option B, 68 percent of respondents preferred the lower-priced Option A, with just 32 percent preferring Option C. Adding Option B back into the lineup changed everything. Now 86 percent chose the higher-priced Option C, only 16 percent chose the lower-priced Option A, and no one chose Option B. It seems that Option B led people who would normally spend less to see value in spending more.

Decoy offers rely on what behavioral economists call *anchoring*. The idea is to fix an expectation in customer minds so that when something better comes along they can more readily see its value.

A simple test illustrates. Show subjects a printed number. Then show them a product and ask them to estimate its price. You will find that those who saw a higher number will estimate higher prices than those who saw a lower one. This holds true even when you tell them not to let the number influence them.

For behavioral economists, decoy offers are merely interesting. For marketers, they're an opportunity. While the purpose of an *incentive offer* is to increase *response*, the purpose of a *decoy offer* is to increase the average *purchase amount*.

One of our corporate clients had good reason to believe his customer base was as big as it was going to get. His business was profitable, but he was troubled by how often established customers purchased against their best interest by looking only at price tags. We tried adding two higher-priced options alongside his popular, low-priced one. The new options were identical to one another in price, but one was clearly a better value. The result? Most of his customers shifted from the low-price option to the more valuable of the high-priced ones.

We recently tested a decoy offer for a retail service industry client who charges by the piece. His internal costs dropped significantly for orders of seven or more pieces, so it was worth it to him to offer deep discounts for eight or more. The average order remained at about five pieces. We came up with a decoy offer designed not to win new customers but to increase volume among existing ones. The promotion offered three options. Option 1: Save five percent on orders of up to six pieces. Option 2: Save 20 percent for seven to 12 pieces. Option 3: Save 25 percent on 13 pieces or more.

Astute readers will have picked up on the noticeably greater savings leap between Options 1 and 2 than between Options 2 and 3. That was intentional. Option 3 was the decoy offer. Its job was to make the generous leap in savings between Options 1 and 2 shine. The decision was in part based on our client's data, which showed that orders of 13 or more pieces were rare. In fact, there was some doubt as to whether 13 or more pieces was even realistic.

The result? For the first time in this client's experience, 73 percent of orders were for seven or more pieces. Orders for six or fewer pieces dropped to 27 percent.

Post-analysis revealed a bonus surprise. Remember our doubts about 13 pieces? Dead wrong. Over 25 percent of total orders were for 13 or more.

There is nothing sneaky about decoy offers. What they do is dramatize the advantage of a deal that is in your customer's best interest.

Try it. You may increase spend and better serve your customer. And you may, as we did, happen upon useful information you weren't expecting.

Chapter 23

The At-A-Glance Test

Most people decide to read or not to read an ad with little more than perfunctory look. That perfunctory look is your only opportunity to win interest. To increase your chances of success, be sure your work passes the At-A-Glance Test.

To pass the At-A-Glance test, advertising must communicate three important pieces of information the moment a pair of eyes falls upon it. With one look and without effort, recipients must instantly be able to ascertain (1) whether your message is relevant to them, (2) what's for sale, and (3) why they should want it.

On the heels of those three points, recipients should be able to easily find who you are and how to connect with you. Locations, phone numbers, and web addresses should jump out. On a printed page, that usually means placing them at the bottom of the layout, right under your logo. Online, it means placing them near the top. (Avoid the temptation of making your logo the largest element. Your logo is only important once you have interested readers in what you can do for them.)

Being creative is fun, and creativity is an important tool for winning attention, but be careful not to obscure your message behind too much or irrelevant creativity. Visual elements and word play should telegraph what's for sale, not divert attention from it. Contrary to popular lore, most readers do not pause to unravel enigmatic advertisements, but summarily give up on them. Directness and clarity work best for communicating at a glance. It follows that they sell more.

Being honest with yourself when applying the At-A-Glance Test to your own work isn't as easy as it might seem. Once you have created your advertising, its message is obvious to you. The trick is to figure out whether it is obvious to people hardly paying attention.

A good way to apply the At-A-Glance Test is to seek out fresh pairs of eyes and let them no more than glance at the layout. Do not ask what they "think of" the ad. Instead, ask: What was the message? Who does it target? Why should they want what's for sale?

Do this and you'll have a better handle on how your work will fare when it ventures into the real world.

Chapter 24

Advice for Restaurateurs

Due respect, but it's not the food

When restaurateurs* retain us, I ask, "What is it about your place that brings people in?" Invariably the answer is, "Our food."

Wrong.

The number one driver of a restaurant's business is its location. It needs to be easily visible from the road, even to those not looking for it. It should be where there is plenty of customer traffic. It should be easy to get in and out of. Ideally, you should plop it down near other, successful restaurants. There are four reasons for that. One is that many people choose a restaurant by going where there are lots of them and then deciding which one appeals. That's the idea behind food courts in malls. Another is that when neighboring, competing places fill up, you'll get some of their overflow. Another is that you will benefit when your neighboring restaurants advertise, because people who come to see them will also see you. Still another is that, because location matters, established, successful restaurants nearby speak well for that spot.

The number two driver is the experience you create for your customers. Food is, of course, part of the experience, but the first thing customers "taste" is the look and feel of the place: theme, lighting, interior design, menu layout, cleanliness, service, the appearance and manners of your people, and presentation. Customers taste with their other senses long before your cuisine sets foot in their mouth. The more visceral appeal your place has, the better the food will taste. Menu hint: Food photography is an art. If you can't afford a pro, having no photos at all is usually better than taking your own.

Food comes in third, and not as important a third as you think. People frequent places where location and ambience offer great appeal, even when the food is mediocre. To name a few: Cracker Barrel, Old Spaghetti Factory, Cheesecake Factory, Chili's, California Pizza Kitchen, Applebee's. None of these has great food. Meanwhile, restaurants with superior fare in a poor location and who give less thought to the experience languish.

If you have a lousy location and little distinguishing ambience, you're not necessarily doomed. It's just that one dilly of an uphill battle awaits you.

Here's a hint: Before you open a restaurant where another has failed, make sure that the location wasn't the main culprit. And before you get to making recipes, remember that your real product is a place with the kind of look and feel that people enjoy.

*Remember to omit the *n*. It's *restaurateur*, not *restauranteur.*

Chapter 25

How Two Unknown Authors Outsold 98% of Published Books

"A Polygamist In Your Inbox"

Not many authors enjoy being told they need to be marketers. They will tell you that theirs is a higher calling. They are artists, storytellers, expositors of human nature.

Fine, but an author unread is none of the above. Successful authoring requires successful marketing. Here are some marketing rules Joanne Hanks and I followed in creating and marketing her memoir, *"It's Not About the Sex" My Ass: Confessions of an Ex-Mormon Ex-Polygamist Ex-Wife*. We are grateful to report that as of this writing it has outsold 98 percent of all published books.

Rule 1: Write a book that people want to read

When Joanne approached me about co-writing the story of her years in a Mormon-based polygamist cult, which she and her then-husband left mainstream Mormonism to join, my Inner Marketer demurred. Despite the public's appetite for "Sister Wives" and "Big Love," the category is overrun. Amazon lists 2,236 titles, most of them languishing unsold. I had no interest in adding one more.

But then Joanne shared a few nutty tales. Thanks to time's healing power, she could laugh at them, which in turn made it okay for me to laugh, too. It dawned on us that no one had yet exposed polygamy by means of humor and sarcasm. We had found a niche. Ours would not be "just another plyg book" after all.

Rule 2: Timing matters

We wanted to capitalize on the fact that (perhaps you heard) the 2012 Republican presidential candidate, Mitt Romney, was a Mormon. Rather than lose time shopping the manuscript, we chose to publish on-demand and e-editions.

There were pros and cons. On-demand and e-publishing yield higher royalties while making a book instantly available worldwide. But we wouldn't have a branded publisher backing the project, and we had no advertising budget. We decided to move ahead. Printed copies and e-editions became available in August, 2012.

Rule 3: A solid book has a solid brand

Joanne is mission-driven. She wants to crush cults, help women who defer their decision-making learn to stand on their own feet, and promote critical thinking. She also has a sense of humor. These traits coalesced into a powerful brand consistent in tone, theme, attitude, and purpose.

A well-branded book needs a well-branded title. *"It's Not About the Sex" My Ass* came to us as we discussed the tendency of polygamists to piously deny that their lifestyle is about sex. Next, we needed a subtitle to crystallize its meaning. *Confessions of an Ex-Mormon, Ex-Polygamist, Ex-Wife* seemed to do the trick. We mocked up a cover and found that people instantly got it. Even better, most belly-laughed.

The brand survived its first challenge when the on-demand service we'd selected insisted on changing *Ass* to *A***. We felt the change would weaken the brand promise of blunt, in-your-face snark that the contents deliver. The service stood firm, so we switched to a competing service.

Rule 4: Use social media and your personal contacts

Owning a marketing firm doesn't mean you're rich. At least, it doesn't in my case. We now had a book that was available in paperback, hardcover, Kindle, iBooks, and Nook, and we had an ad budget of zero.

We created our official website and then asked—begged, really—Facebook friends to like and share. I emailed business contacts across the country in hopes of enlisting help and, with luck, endorsements. The subject line I used was "A polygamist in your inbox."

Buzz began overnight. "Best title ever," posted many on Facebook, LinkedIn, Pinterest, and elsewhere. "You deserve an award for best subject line," wrote a nationally recognized direct marketing expert. Whew. Not giving in to asterisks was, it seemed, the right choice. Sales came in from all over the U.S., and from Canada, the UK, Australia, and Europe.

Rule 5: Be damned lucky

Things started happening. A well-known Australian podcast and two popular American podcasts featured Joanne. The UK's highest-circulation women's magazine interviewed her. In Utah, which, you may have heard, has a large Mormon population, the market's most popular morning radio show invited Joanne to the studio and featured her for an hour.

By accident, I learned that Tom Flynn, editor of *Free Inquiry* magazine, had an interest in Mormon lore. I sent him a copy, not without trepidation. If he liked the book, thousands of readers might order it. If he didn't, thousands would go nowhere near it. "Simply delightful," his full-page rave review read, to our relief. A few weeks later, an Association for Mormon Letters review said, "Of the dozens of recent books authored by those who escaped from polygamous groups, this one is unique and worth a read."

With each event, sales shot up. On Amazon, that creates an upward spiral. By the time the national media featured Rebecca Musser's *The Witness Wore Red*, Amazon was listing *"It's Not About the Sex" My Ass* one or two titles below hers. Sales reached a record high.

As this volume goes to press, *"It's Not About the Sex" My Ass* has been out four years. It has sold in the thousands and shows no signs of slowing.

Looking back

It's easy to look back and claim that we were smart. But had we misjudged the public's appetite for polygamy told with sarcastic humor ... had Facebook friends not supported us ... had interviewers and reviewers not liked the book ... had the market suddenly tired of the topic ... had *Ass* instead of *A*** been a mistake ... our book would have languished.

For that matter, had I not had the good fortune to meet Joanne, and had she not made me laugh, there would be no book in the first place. So it is that we gratefully acknowledge Step 5.

Nonetheless, serendipity needs something to work with. Overlook Steps 1 through 4, and Step 5 will not have so much as a fighting chance. Budding authors take heed.

Chapter 26

B2B Telephone Prospecting

9 tips for getting them not to hate you

Have your pitchforks and torches at the ready: I admit to prospecting for clients by phone. It is how I have landed more than a few. Moreover, more than one business-to-business (B2B) prospector has brought useful services to me.

There is nothing wrong with B2B teleprospecting provided you follow a few simple rules. Here, in no particular order, are some that work for me.

1. Don't pretend it's not a sales call. Do not stoop to "I'm not calling to sell you anything." We both know that, whether now or later, a sale is the ultimate objective. Denying as much will only insult your prospect's intelligence. I have had success with this uber-honest opener: "Brace yourself: This is a sales call." It usually draws a chuckle, followed by, "Go for it."

2. Obtain permission to pitch. Before presuming to charge ahead with my spiel, I ask, "Am I catching you at a good time?" That gives the prospect an out, but you know what? None has yet taken it. They appreciate it when you respect their time. Often, those who can talk will hear you out, and those who cannot will give you a time to call back. Of course, if they tell you to get lost and not to call back, get lost and don't call back. They are saving their and your time.

3. Be nice to admins. Don't think that acting abrupt and important will make an admin quiver in fear and forward you to the boss. Admins deal with the likes of you every day. You will stand out from the others if you treat that person like an equal and enlist his or her aid.

Here's an approach that led to landing one of the biggest clients of my career: "I realize that your job is to protect Mr. A from people like me. Trouble is, what my company does is something I am sure would interest him. Is there anything you can do to help me?" With a bit of surprise in her voice, she replied, "I'll do my best for you." And she did.

4. Be ready with a long, medium, and short summary of how you can help the prospect. Do not waste time talking about how great your company is. Focus on what you propose to do for your prospect.

5. Do your homework. I am utterly turned off when a caller doesn't know what my company does. Some dopes even ask outright, "So, what does RESPONSE Agency do?" If you call knowing nothing about my business, your claim that your company or product can help me is an empty one.

6. Get to the point. Don't waste an executive's time. Avoid long intros, and keep background info as short as possible.

7. Know when to let go. The moment it becomes clear that you're not going to make a sale, graciously thank the prospect and end the call. That's good manners. If manners fail to impress you, consider that a prospect who likes you may someday call you back or refer you.

Note to Positive Mental Attitude junkies: "Know when to let go" is not the same as "give up easily." Spare me your scolding and maybe I'll hold off writing about just how lame and often counterproductive the Positive Mental Attitude industry is. For now.

One more thing. If there is no interest, do NOT offer to send literature and do NOT give the prospect your phone number "just in case you have any questions." It is a waste of your company's money and a sure sign of an amateur.

8. Have an objective when you call. What do you hope to accomplish by the end of the call? Everything you say should advance the conversation in that direction.

9. Don't farm out high-level B2B prospecting calls. Farming out calls out is okay for a consumable like toner. High-level calls are another matter altogether. Outside callers cannot not know your company well enough to field questions of any depth. Besides, it's a little ironic if not a little insulting to interrupt a busy executive with a call that wasn't worth your time to place.

Chapter 27

Using PR to Stay Out of Trouble

Too many CEOs think that a public relations department's job is to spin a decision, action, statement, or policy so that the public will like it, not notice it, or, at least, not dislike it.

Sometimes that is needful and possible. More often, it only makes a scapegoat of the PR department after some moronic corporate action has blown up beyond recovery.

An effective PR department should have the savvy* and wherewithal, and you must ensure them access to you and immunity from your umbrage, to warn you before you do something irreparably stupid. Else, you deprive yourself of a valuable opportunity to keep your foot from ending up in your mouth.

Myriad bad examples abound. I could cite one that popped up in my home town not long ago, but I'd rather share a positive example. Happily, I happen to have one.

One of my clients, a multi-state operation, had been taking a beating in the press. (Between you and me, it was deserved.) Over lunch, their marketing VP told me they were going to pull all of their advertising from a TV station that had been particularly aggressive in exposing them.

I am not a PR person, but I didn't get to be good at marketing by not understanding a thing or two about how minds work. I said, "The station is portraying you as a big, power-ful, heartless corporation. What you propose will validate that and elevate them to martyr status. On tonight's news, they will accuse your giant corporation of using economic pressure to keep their brave reporters from telling the truth about you."

The marketing VP returned to headquarters and convinced the CEO not to pull their advertising.

• How do you screen for savvy? I have seen more than my share of PR and marketing "professionals" who, not knowing their right hand from their left, float awful ideas and kill great ones. A good starting point is to look for PR and marketing people who rely more on evidence than on gut. Good luck finding them. When you do, swoop them up and pay them too much to want to leave.

Chapter 28

How the Internet Improves Commercials

Computers and personal devices let you do something your TV never could. Namely, skip a commercial that fails to appeal within five seconds. It also lets advertisers do something they couldn't before, namely, count how many surfers skip their commercials.

Some advertisers let you opt out of a commercial after a few seconds. Smart. Others prefer to make you sit through their commercial, like it or not. Big mistake. Force-feeding is a lousy way to win friends. The nature of the medium pretty much neutralizes force-feeding anyway, since surfers can kill the sound and busy themselves in another window until your commercial has played out. Most important, advertisers who don't let you skip miss a valuable opportunity to make more effective commercials. Every advertiser understands the importance of hooking viewer attention from the get-go. The skip option lets advertisers know if they're succeeding or if they need to try another approach. Internet commercials can reveal overnight what took months and sometimes years to learn in the old TV days.

Viewer control has made the Internet an unforgiving environment for commercials that people don't want to watch.

The advertiser's best solution? Make commercials that people *do* want to watch.

That's a good thing for advertisers and viewers alike. It forces advertisers to produce better work, and it lessens the poor work that viewers have to sit through.

Ads do seem to be improving. Not long ago, I opted out of most ads almost robot-like, unthinking, as a matter of course. No longer. More and more, I tell my cursor, "Hold on; this one looks interesting."

Part Five

What Little I Know About the Loyalty Business

Chapter 29

If You Call It a Loyalty Program, It Isn't.

(Plus: How really to create loyalty)

Here's a tip. Don't call your loyalty program a loyalty program.

For one thing, competent marketers know better than to focus messaging on what they want to say or sell, but rather to focus on what their customers want to hear or buy. I can assure you that nowhere on the Things Customers Want to Hear or Buy List will you find, "To give you my loyalty."

For another, I bet that your program gives customers points toward freebies in return for buying from you. The idea is that they'll spend more dollars more often in order to build up points. I admit to pedantry here, but that's not a loyalty program. It's a frequency and rewards program.

Increased frequency and average amount spent are not the same thing as loyalty. Come on. You're not building loyalty. You're bribing customers to return. No need to take exception at my invoking the B word. Bribing customers is a perfectly legitimate marketing tactic when we're not talking about politicians. American Express Rewards, Marriott Rewards, Delta SkyMiles and others make an art of it. But if you think a bribed customer is a loyal customer, just wait until a competitor with a richer bribe comes along.

Truly loyal customers are loath to leave you. It's more emotional than rational. That makes it hard to measure, but not hard to spot. Look no further than the number of Apple customers who steadfastly resist opportunities to save money on arguably equally capable, non-Apple products. Or the number of Harley riders who would rather die than be seen perched atop anything other than a Hog. Apple, I might point out, has no loyalty or rewards program. Harley-Davidson offers a co-branded Visa Rewards credit card plus gives rewards for online purchases. These may increase the amount spent on gifts and accessories, but neither the credit card nor the rewards program lie at the root of Harley's fierce biker loyalty.

Loyalty is attainable on the small scale, too. The owners of Los Garcia, my favorite Salt Lake City area Mexican restaurant, treat me so well that I feel pangs of guilt at the mere thought of going elsewhere for Mexican food.

Apple-esque, Harley-esque, and Garcia-esque loyalty does not flow from any sort of program. It flows from delivering a consistent, uncommonly positive experience.

Want loyal customers? First be loyal to them.

Chapter 30

Tips on Loyalty

The cost associated with selling to an established customer is usually much lower than that of selling to a first-time customer. So, while acquiring customers is certainly recommended, so is securing the loyalty of customers you already have.

"Loyalty," the umbrella term used for retaining and growing customers, is a burgeoning marketing field with its own best practices. But the basics of attaining loyalty are largely intuitive, which means you can implement many strategies on your own:

Target most-profitable customers. With tracking, you'll soon learn who your most frequent, most profitable customers are. Focusing on keeping and growing best customers is more affordable, and is likely to earn a greater return, than blanketing all (including unprofitable) customers.

Surprise and delight. Unexpected touches work wonders. Even so little as a simple thank-you note has power to impress. Provided, that is, that it doesn't look mass-produced, even if it really is. On occasion, you might also send a gift card, a coupon for free merchandise, an invitation to an event, or offer a better-than-advertised deal.

Privileges impress. According special privileges is a proven way to enhance feelings of loyalty, often with greater effect than giving away freebies. That's because, whether they admit it or not, most people love having a privilege when they know that others don't have it. You might provide your best customers a straight-to-the-CEO email address, spare them a wait in line, reserve them a special parking space, open the store early to accommodate their schedule, offer a free delivery ... your imagination is the limit.

Punch cards. A favorite of coffeehouses and fast food eateries, the punch card tracks purchases until the customer has earned a freebie. The classic use: buy 10 cups of joe or sandwiches, and the next one is free. If you use punch cards, track carefully. Sometimes instead of increasing frequency and loyalty, you end up giving away what you might have sold anyway, and at full price.

A good loyalty program pays for itself. Be sure to maintain a control group that resembles your loyalty group, but that doesn't participate in the program. If the loyalty group produces more average revenue per customer than the control, chances are your program is working.

Chapter 31

Have You Hugged Your Best Customers Lately?

When Valentine's Day rolls around, I cannot help noticing that marketing often resorts to love-and-courtship metaphors. We *woo* and *engage*. We remain *faithful* to brand promises. We build *relationships*.

Let's push the metaphor a step further. After a sale has been—dare I say it?—*consummated*, day-to-day demands threaten to divert our attention, causing us to unwittingly take for granted those who matter most.

So, in the spirit of Valentine's Day, here are a few tips for keeping customer relationships alive. Who knows? Maybe these tips will prove useful at home, too.

1. *Don't shy from the expected.* Some marketers fear that an appreciation strategy may be expected and appear contrived. Indeed it may, but that's hardly an indictment. The greater risk is *failing* to do the expected, as anyone who served time in the doghouse after forgetting Valentine's Day or an anniversary can attest.

2. *Go for the unexpected.* One day I received a note, seemingly out of the blue, over the signature of the president of the Book of the Month Club. A free book coupon was enclosed. "You're a good customer," the note said in essence, "and I

wanted to say thanks." Even though I know a hidden-points trigger program when I see one, I felt recognized and flattered. I also bought lots more books.

3. *Make it personal.* Perhaps ironically, today's technology can make mailings of any volume feel personal. Take advantage of that! Address your customer by name. Shoot for a warm tone. And for once, resist the urge to blather about a commitment to excellence.

4. *Remember the power of just "thank you."* When I left a surprise bonus check with a note of thanks on an employee's chair, he choked up because of the note. Yeah, he'd seen the check. "But the note," he sniffled.

5. *Be picky.* It rarely makes economic sense to send remembrances to all customers. Acknowledging the 20 percent who likely account for the 80 percent of your success can pay out big.

6. *Keep going.* You cannot build and reward loyalty with infrequent contact. To remember hearing from you at all, most customers will need to hear from you often.

I suppose I should concede that marketing doesn't limit itself to love metaphors. We also seem to like war metaphors. We aim at *targets*, use *guerilla tactics*, and wage *campaigns*. Maybe I'll write about that on Veteran's Day.

Chapter 32

Loyal Customers and Proposing on the Serengeti

Ethan knew how to propose. On a trip to the Serengeti, his back to a spectacular sunset, he knelt before Jessica, produced a lovely ring, and begged for her hand. So it was that one of the RESPONSE Agency's best employees returned from her vacation engaged.

I suppose Ethan could have skipped the whole Serengeti sunset thing. He could have cornered Jessica at a local café and said, "Because we appreciate your being a valued significant other ..." If that strikes you as the more efficient approach, you may have a promising career with a company that mistakes sending emails and snail mail to "valued customers like you" for loyalty marketing. For the rest of you, here are some tips.

Something odd happens when marketers try to create loyal customer relationships. Namely, they forget everything they know about loyalty and relationships. You earn personal friends by treating people with fairness and thoughtfulness, being reliable, telling the truth and keeping promises—not by wearing a tagline that says "I care," awarding points toward merchandise, or offering rebates for a two-year contract. Taglines, rewards and contracts are powerful and have their place—in no way am I telling you not to use them—but a business that wants genuine loyalty should first take a look at its practices.

Nothing says "lazy copywriter" like "valued customer." Banish that term from your marketing lexicon. Use your creativity to show, not tell, customers that they matter. Speaking of which...

Warm and fuzzy is a good start. A sincere "thank you" in the mail is a welcome surprise. Be sure it doesn't appear mass-produced, even if it is. Print it on your personal letterhead ("Monarch" size makes a nice impression), address the customer by name, use a stamp (no indicia in this case), and add your signature in blue.

Beyond warm and fuzzy. To keep succeeding notes fresh, enclose something of value. Free merchandise is good. On the less costly side, you can enclose article reprints (be sure to obtain the rights), press releases ("I want you to hear this from me before you see it in the paper"), offers of better-than-advertised deals, smart shopping tips, and so on.

Privileges motivate. There's nothing quite so heady as knowing you have a privilege that others don't have. You might provide your best customers a straight-to-the-CEO email address, spare them a wait in line, reserve them the best parking spaces ... your imagination is the limit.

Understand the difference between loyalty and frequency. This is loyalty: When it's safer to broach religion or politics than to suggest to a Harley rider a switch to Kawasaki. Frequency, which is easier to measure, may or may not indicate loyalty. By contrast, a mere frequent customer may only be a coupon-surfer and easy prey for the first competitor who undercuts you.

Rewards programs can build frequency and profitability. Two cautions are in order: (1) There are limits to the number of programs in which people will participate. (2) They're trickier than they look. A homemade program could end up costing you money and embarrassment. Before you get too far, consult with one or more pros.

A good loyalty program pays for itself. Whether yours is a complex rewards system or a simple thank-you note program, maintain a control group that resembles your loyalty group. If the loyalty group produces more revenue than the control, chances are your program is working.

Is loyalty for you? Loyalty marketing is based on the idea that selling to established customers costs less than creating new customers. This is often true, but not always. Before you invest in a loyalty program, be sure your company will truly benefit from having one. Not every relationship requires a Serengeti sunset.

Part Six

A Marketer's Guide to Surviving Intuition

Chapter 33

A Critical Dose Of Critical Thinking

Try this self-test to see if you were born with critical thinking skills.

1. Mark down two points if you're human, one if you're not human, and zero if you're unsure.

2. Total your points.

3. A score of two indicates that, even if you're a good critical thinker, you probably weren't born that way. If you scored one or less, be careful whom you tell.

Critical thinking is a process for avoiding being fooled. It consists of knowing how to separate fact from fiction, and how to separate conclusions that follow from the facts from conclusions that don't.

If you think you can neither be fooled nor fool yourself—sorry, there's no tactful way to say this—you're being naive. There's a reason that scientists employ safeguards such as blind testing, strict controls, replication, and peer review. Even their highly trained minds are subject to being fooled, including fooling themselves. Those who dispense with the safeguards risk public failure and embarrassment. Look no further than Stanley Pons and Martin Fleischmann of fizzled cold fusion fame.

So perhaps we marketers should think twice before deeming ourselves immune. Indeed, we fool ourselves all the time.

Consider arguments typically used to establish marketing success: sales are up; focus group participants liked the ads; phone research showed an increase in the number of people who said they'd purchase; web hits rose; the video went viral; the campaign won awards; post-campaign research showed an increase in awareness; and, not to be overlooked, someone's gut intuition just knows it's a great campaign.

All it takes to call the above into question is a bit of critical thinking. It's as simple as stepping back and saying, "Just a darned minute. What does the evidence really show?" A sales increase can result from factors other than advertising; focus group research is not predictive; people say they'll purchase but do not follow through; web hits aren't sales; a message can go viral and not sell; failed campaigns win awards; and awareness can be attained without attaining sales. And gut intuition? Be honest. Your gut tells you the sun orbits Earth.

Yet who can blame anyone for buying those fallacious arguments? We have heard them throughout our careers. They *seem* to make sense. And we want to believe our stuff works. But if we want to *know*, regardless of what we wish to *believe*, we would do well to engage in some critical thinking.

Suppose you want to know whether your marketing and not some other factor was responsible for a sales increase. As a critical thinker, you might begin by asking, "What would it take to convince me that the marketing *didn't* work?" If your answer is, "Nothing, because I know I'm right," you're not thinking critically, but dogmatically.

As a critical thinker, you might say, "Suppose I divide a representative sample of my market into Group 1 and Group 2, taking care to keep them alike in terms of demographics and psychographics. I'll expose only Group 1 to the marketing so that, to the best of my knowledge, there will be no other differences between the groups. If Group 1 purchases more than Group 2, I can reasonably conclude that my marketing is responsible. If the groups perform equally, I can conclude that my marketing made no difference. And, heaven forbid, should Group 2 outperform Group 1, I'll conclude that my marketing is hurting sales."

There is no such thing as an unbiased human being, so it's important to conduct a *blind* test. Do not let either Group know about the other, what you hope to learn, or even that a test is afoot. Knowledge of any of those things will make them self-conscious and affect their behavior.

Want to get more scientific? *Double-blind* the test. Ensure that whoever tracks the Groups' purchases doesn't know which Group is which. That helps exclude any bias a data gatherer may have.

Want to get even MORE scientific? *Triple-blind* the test. Make sure that whoever compiles and interprets the data doesn't know one Group from the other, either.

Flukes happen, but consistent results are highly reliable indicators. That means it's a good idea to repeat the test two or three times with new, equally valid samples.

A critical approach isn't for people who want to prove themselves right. It's for people who want to *find out what's right*. It brims with advantages. It reduces error and self-delusion. Every test leads to learning.

The obvious benefit, of course, is that you'll know—not just think you know—what's working, so you can do more of it. Equally important, you'll know what's not working, so you can modify, replace, or retire it instead of throwing good money after bad.

All of which would seem to indicate that critical thinking can be critical to your continued success and employment.

Chapter 34

Marketing, Soap, and the Scientific Method

Note to parents: Washing your kid's mouth out with soap doesn't prevent cussing. I know because of a test my son conducted when he was six years old. Upon a repeat-offender friend's mouth being washed out with soap for the umpteenth time, my son came home, applied soap to his own mouth, and proceeded to see if he could say "damn." Out came the word, sharp and clear. Another myth was busted.

Little did he know that he'd used the scientific method. Indeed, said method isn't the exclusive domain of scientists. If a six-year-old can use it to sort fact from fancy, presumably a grown-up marketer might profit from giving it a try.

Forget how tedious your grade school teacher made the scientific method sound. I'll put it in Real People-ese. You start with a hunch ("Soaping a mouth prevents cussing"); you make an earnest attempt to prove your hunch *wrong* ("If that's so, then I shouldn't be able to swear after soaping my mouth"); and you draw a conclusion from the results ("I was still able to say 'damn,' so the hunch was most likely wrong").

Suppose you want to display high-margin impulse items where your retail customers are most likely to browse. You may think you know the ideal spot, but why not apply the scientific method? You can develop hunches by discreetly watching and tallying customer traffic patterns. Then you can test them by placing the display in each promising location and, again, watching and counting. As consistent patterns emerge, you'll be able to draw reliable conclusions.

Research genius and author of *Why We Buy* Paco Underhill built his career on doing such observations. It is thanks to him that we know that most customers who enter your store will shuffle off to their right. They will, that is, if they drive on the right. People who live in the UK, Bahamas, and other drive-on-the-left countries tend to move to their left.

Underhill has also shown that people linger longer at displays placed where other shoppers are less likely to brush them as they pass by, and that you'll sell more women's clothing if you give the men in their lives a comfortable chair outside the dressing rooms along with a TV tuned to ESPN.

That's not the kind of information you'll obtain by asking customers their habits. People who think they can predict their own behavior, which is most people, are mistaken. This was born out by a test I conducted myself. The challenge was to choose between two covers for a romantic music CD. One cover was black with a red heart in the middle. The other featured a golden sunset cliché. In intercept interviews, nearly everyone scoffed at the sunset and expressed a strong preference for the sexier black cover. Next, I quit asking and started watching. I stacked the two versions side-by-side on a tray, told people that the CDs were identical, and offered to let them take one free. I did not reveal that I was testing, and I didn't ask for opinions. Each time someone chose a CD, I replaced it to keep the stacks equal. I also rotated the stacks in case people were biased toward right or left. The results were eye-opening. Nearly everyone had expressed a preference for the black cover, but when it came time to take one home, *everyone* grabbed the sunset version. Cliché and all.

The more I resort to the scientific method, the more I am surprised at what I learn. Testing has shown that I am no marketing clairvoyant. I was rooting for the losing CD design. Likewise, I was certain that offering a free entertainment center remote control would outperform offering a free flashlight, but in a series of tests the flashlight handily won. For a university alumni association fund-raiser, I expected a mission-centered appeal to outperform a member-benefits appeal, but a test revealed no difference. Further testing showed that response rose only when the school's football team won games. Since fixing sporting events isn't one of the RESPONSE Agency's core capabilities, there wasn't much I could do with that bit of knowledge.

The fact that outcomes aren't always what you want them to be is why it's important to use the scientific method. Careful testing, observing and tallying are the surest ways to protect against seeing what you hope to see, which may or may not really be there. Even famous, so-called fortune-tellers who claim to be right 90 percent of the time are in fact wrong most of the time, as revealed when anyone bothers to count.

Sadly, few people do bother to count, which is one of the reasons these frauds stay in business.

Not all marketers want facts. I know many who readily disqualify all inconvenient data. Still others exhibit remarkable creativity when it comes to twisting data to make them appear to say what they do not.

I recall one enterprising fellow who managed to convince himself and his not inconsiderable company that a solitary customer who responded to an offer, amid 9,000 who did not, justified continued spending on a program that clearly wasn't working.

Someone should have washed out his mouth with soap.

Chapter 35

The Trouble with Gut-Driven Marketing

Excerpted with the author's permission from the book Prove It Before You Promote It. *I happen to be the author, so obtaining permission was not difficult.*

Most people know that a ten-ton iron ball falls as fast as a half-pound iron ball. But in earlier times, any fool "knew" that heavier objects fell faster.

How they knew is instructive. Scientific questions in those days were not settled by testing but by philosophizing. It was true that heavy objects fell faster, scholars reasoned, because any fool knew they did. Thus this pseudo-fact, canonized by Aristotle himself, reigned as truth for over a millennium.

To change things, it took a skeptic, whom tradition identifies as Galileo, to do something revolutionary: conduct a test. He dropped two iron balls, one considerably heavier than the other, from atop a tall building, which tradition identifies as the Leaning Tower of Pisa.

I'd like to tell you that from the moment the iron balls simultaneously hit the ground a new theory prevailed, but that's not what happened. Human beings have a long history of not being impressed by something so unconvincing as solid evidence. You may recall the fate of poor Galileo, his evidence for heliocentrism notwithstanding.

Enlightened age?

Today we have the scientific method, thanks to which most of us no longer believe that flies spontaneously generate from decaying meat, fresh air is unhealthy, or the sun circles the earth. But people still cling to unsupportable gut feelings. Witness those who wear a lucky hat when golfing, consult horoscopes before traveling, wear magnets to ward off arthritis, and abstain from chocolate to prevent acne.

Do not tell them that their beliefs are unscientific unless you're ready for a fruitless argument. You'll find that they won't care about evidence, they'll counter with anecdotes, or they'll become belligerent.

Millennia after Galileo, people still don't like it when you question what any fool knows.

Marketing and intuition

With the possible exception of abstaining from chocolate, many erroneous beliefs are arguably harmless. But some are not. It's one thing to wear a silly golf hat. It's another to stake marketing dollars on one campaign because it "feels right" or to reject another because it "feels wrong."

Yet every day, marketers do exactly that. They make big decisions using gastrointestinal enlightenment as their guide. Then, to ensure that everyone is duly impressed with the higher authority of their lower half, they justify the decision with, "And my gut"—pause for effect—"is never wrong."

Gut success ratios

There would be nothing objectionable about gut-driven marketing if guts were always or even usually right. They are neither. At best, the ratio of correct to incorrect gut-driven decisions is fifty-fifty.

Here's why. For every gut that turns out to be right, another necessarily turns out to be wrong. Fred Smith's gut felt that Federal Express would succeed, but his Yale professor's gut disagreed. George Martin's gut believed in the Beatles, but the Decca record company's Dick Rowe's gut led him to infamously say, "Guitar bands are on their way out." Henry Ford's gut felt that Americans wanted affordable automobiles, but his early partners' guts didn't.

I don't find 50 percent odds encouraging, but if you do, I must confess that your gut's odds are really much lower. The above examples are based on successful ventures. Consider the number that bomb: failed products like Edsel and New Coke, deserted retail outlets, movies no one sees, and bankrupt entrepreneurs, to name a few. More ideas flop than fly, yet behind every flop was a gut that assured a believer, "It'll work."

What about guts that predict failure? Aren't they right most of the time? Sorry to disappoint, but while killing ideas means avoiding failures, it also means avoiding breakthroughs.

Thomas Edison missed out by not going with alternating current, Henry Ford lost ground by not offering color choices, and the founders of Starbucks rejected an opportunity to increase profits by selling brewed coffee (only after Howard Schultz bought them out and became CEO did Starbucks enter the café business). Dismissing opportunities out of hand is risky in its own right. With the number of ideas that never make it to market, there is no way of knowing how many early abortive plans might have turned out to be the Beatles.

Your gut isn't the exception

If you think that your gut defies the odds and is right most of the time, I'd suggest four possibilities: hindsight bias, incomplete information, tossing coins, and reading clues.

Hindsight bias is the tendency to remember what confirms and not what contradicts. People whose guts are right "most of the time" overlook, often unwittingly, the times they were wrong. Incomplete information is another problem. In some organizations, saying the boss was mistaken is career-limiting, so news of failures never makes it to the top. Information fails to surface for other reasons, too. If you feel but can't verify that your advertising produces sales, you really don't know if your ads are working or not. You just think you know.

If your gut really is right most of the time—it's possible— you may be a lucky coin flipper. In his book *Science Friction: Where the Known Meets the Unknown*, Michael Shermer observes:

"If you conduct a coin-flipping experiment and record heads or tails, you will shortly encounter streaks. How many streaks and how long? On average and in the long run, you will flip five heads or tails in a row once in every thirty-two sequences of five tosses."

If your gut really has been right most of the time, beware. The next toss may betray you.

It's also possible that, instead of having an infallible gut, you're adept at reading clues. In college I amazed a young woman I'd just met by identifying her religion, discerning that she was a musician, and then, after promising to name her musical instrument, correctly identifying her as a singer.

Pegging her as a musician was a lucky guess. A musician myself and not a little twitterpated by her, I was grasping for common ground. As for her religion and instrument, I read the clues. I saw a religious symbol on her keychain. When I promised to name her instrument, she traded a conspiratorial, "now we have him" look with her friend, which suggested to me that she was a vocalist.

I hesitate to bring up clue-reading, because you may say, "Fine. Call it gut intuition or reading clues. Either way, I'm never wrong." But hindsight makes it hard to distinguish clue-reading from whimsy. Did your gut tell you a job interview went well, were you attuned to the interviewer's positive body language, or did you simply guess right? And reading clues is subject to error. The brightest people misread clues (mental health experts who confuse pseudo dementia for Alzheimer's disease), fail to see clues (parents oblivious to kids on drugs), see non-existent clues (WMDs in Iraq), and let ego mislead (male CEOs who think young women at the company party want to dance with them). You may read clues well, but don't bet your marketing budget on it.

Trading guts for brains

You may ask, what exactly should you bet your marketing budget on? Didn't you work your way into your job using your skills, experience, and judgment?

But that's just it: I'm not asking you to check your judgment at the door. I'm asking you to overrule your gut in favor of good judgment. Judgment doesn't leap to conclusions or stubbornly cling to the unsupportable. Judgment seeks facts. It questions, researches, hypothesizes, experiments, and observes.

If this is beginning to sound less like marketing and more like science, good. Marketing that succeeds on the experimental level has been shown to have high odds of succeeding on the larger scale. That's because, though the behavior of humans as individuals can be all over the board, group behavior tends to be fairly consistent. So the more scientifically you approach marketing, the more you will increase your marketing effectiveness.

Try it. Come up with a marketing hypothesis. Devise a marketing experiment where you can watch, unobserved, how people react. Thanks to marketers who do just that, our industry already knows a great deal. We know that "click here to contact us" works better than "contact us"; that more people call toll-free numbers during late-night TV; that a letter in an envelope will usually outsell a solo brochure; that Web surfers prefer clicking on links displayed in blue; and more.

Testing reveals much on an individual basis, too. For one client, testing showed us the best way to upgrade customer commitment. For another, it isolated a strategy that attracts more profitable, longer-term customers. And for another, it showed us how to cut acquisition costs by sixty percent. All from testing, and all before committing major dollars. By the time our clients were ready to spend big dollars, they had proven, projectable strategies.

In learning to approach marketing scientifically, you needn't start from scratch. In particular, direct marketers have been testing for centuries. Read direct response trade publications. Devour books written by direct response legends. And track results of your own work. Before long, you'll base marketing decisions on experience and observation instead of on what your gut says.

Let empirical evidence and hard numbers guide your choices, and remember that instinct deserves about as much a place in your marketing arsenal as that golf hat.

Chapter 36

Intuition Wars

Sometimes intuition serves us well. When intuition warns us to step away from a snake making a rattling sound, to keep our distance from the edge of a cliff, or not to eat something that smells rotten, one must give intuition its due.

But experiencing too many right intuitive hunches in a row has its down side. It can lead us to believe that our first reactions are always right. In marketing, where people don't always act the way you might expect, too much reliance on your own intuition can lead you to sabotage your own results.

Veterans of what I like to call Intuition Wars know what I mean. For soldiers yet to visit the front, here's an example. When a well-respected private college asked my agency to recruit MBA students, an Intuition War ensued the moment we presented a classic direct mail strategy. According to the client's intuition, no one would read a four-page sales letter; the copy style was too ... too ... "marketing-y"; and for a $50,000 degree program, a $20 gift incentive wouldn't motivate intelligent, MBA-quality people, but insult them.

If you're experienced in direct response marketing, I needn't defend to you the value of long copy, persuasive language, and a strong incentive offer. But I had to defend it to them. At that moment, over a hundred years of proven direct response tactics went up against the intuition of an entire liberal arts college faculty, including marketing and advertising professors. Who was I, with a measly baccalaureate and at the time only 20 years of experience, to argue with a roomful of PhDs?

But argue I did. I convinced them to let the letter and language stand, and to test the gift offer on half of the mailing list. When the gift offer version produced four times as many applicants as the no-offer version, the college, grudgingly but to their credit, continued with the winning version. Over the next two years, they spent about $40,000 in printing and postage, and generated about $1.5 million dollars in tuition.

Had the college's collective intuition prevailed, they would have effectively wasted 75 cents of every marketing dollar they spent on the campaign. For marketers about to stick a tentative toe in the waters of direct marketing, this suggests some important lessons.

1. Don't trust your intuition. I realize this advice flies in the face of PMA gurus who tell you to go with your gut and Star Wars junkies who want you to trust the Force. But gut intuition is often wrong. Consider IBM Chairman Thomas Watson who famously said in 1943, "I think there is a world market for maybe five computers." He was no rare exception, and your intuition is no better.

2. Beware your personal comfort zone. It's not unusual for proven tactics to make the uninitiated uncomfortable. Direct response strategies are often the antithesis of popular advertising. But it's important to remember that direct response tactics became established only by proving their worth. Rather than ask, "Is the headline cheesy?"—whatever "cheesy" means—ask, "Is this the kind of headline that experience shows tends to work?" If the answer is yes, tell your comfort zone that you'll be staying someplace else for a while.

3. *Trust what works for other direct marketers.* When I was new to this business, I studied what seasoned direct marketers did, paying particular attention to what they did repeatedly. When direct marketers stuck with the same commercial, direct mail package, or web page ad nauseam over time, I took it—correctly, it turned out—for a sign that what they were doing was working. The more I copied what I saw them do, the more my results went up.

5. *Conduct your own tests.* Proven techniques notwithstanding, every case is unique. What's the best way to present your product? What incentive will motivate the most response? Which presentation will work best? These are not questions of opinion, but of discovery. Embrace classic strategies, but test and measure the particulars.

6. *Trust results.* I cringe when I recall a client for whom we tested three approaches. When his favorite lost, he declared the test invalid. "I know my customers," he said. "They like what I like." On the contrary, he didn't and they didn't. Avoid assuming that you know what your customers want. Let them show you.

We all have intuitive hunches. They are part of being human, and they often keep us safe. If a rabid coyote shows up in your yard and intuition advises against trying to pet it, go with your gut. But if your gut tells you that proven methods are unprofessional and will not work, I suggest politely overruling it.

Chapter 37

How Odds Get to Be Odds

Most of us know not to publicly say, "I'm smarter than the rest of you," but that doesn't keep us from thinking we are. Research shows that most people believe themselves to be smarter than the average. It also shows that the lesser one's competence in a given area, the more one tends to overestimate oneself. This is known as the Dunning-Kruger Effect.

Come on, admit it. At least some of the time, you think you're smarter than everyone else, or at least that you're smarter or more competent than you really are. To deny it is to deny being human.

I need hardly point out that everyone's being smarter than everyone else presents something of a mathematical impossibility. I would also like to point out the danger of believing you're smarter than everyone else when it comes to making marketing decisions.

To be sure, marketing history has more than its share of visionaries who scoffed at research, laughed in the face of predictive tests, ignored the odds, and went on to great success. Positive thinking enthusiasts make heroes of them and parade their success as the natural and inevitable outcome of damning torpedoes and speeding ahead.

But celebrating people who defied the odds and won overlooks an implicit, sobering reality. Namely, that "odds" refers to "most-likely outcomes." People who defied the odds and won are not models to emulate but exceptions who ought to thank their lucky stars.

Exceptions notwithstanding, it is always safer to bet with than against the odds.

That is, after all, how odds get to be odds.

Chapter 38

Of Giants and Shoulders

Chances are you have heard direct response marketing referred to as "scientific marketing." It is not hyperbole. Testing, re-testing and predicting—the direct marketer's stock-in-trade—are the basis of the Hypothetico-Deductive Model, which scientists generally agree is the essence of science itself. The process by which direct marketers uncover what works and what doesn't, and decide what to keep doing and what never to do again, is the same process by which scientists figure out the universe. Feel free to pull that out of your hat the next time you hope to impress at a cocktail party. Positive results not guaranteed.

Scientists (and direct marketers) routinely publish their findings, which other scientists (and direct marketers) then duplicate, test, and validate or debunk. Then they build upon those findings and share their own. Thus the body of scientific (and direct marketing) knowledge grows to benefit all. Isaac Newton summed it up when he famously said, "If I have seen further, it is by standing on the shoulders of giants."

But giant shoulders provide an advantage only when people bother seeking out and standing atop them. Einstein did not arrive at his Theories of Special and General Relativity in a vacuum. He stood on the shoulders of centuries' worth of physicists whose work came before his. Einstein could think outside the box precisely because he knew what was inside it.

The direct response industry has no shortage of giants with solid shoulders. From nearly two centuries of tracking results, direct marketing has amassed a great deal of proven knowledge as to what works. It stands to reason that by familiarizing yourself with and relying on that knowledge, you can increase ROI faster and spend less money doing it. Overlook it and you risk wasting valuable time and resources while you busy yourself re-inventing the wheel. Or, worse, needlessly and redundantly testing square wheels.

A body of tested, re-tested, predictive knowledge is part of what makes direct response much more than "just another approach." With today's tight budgets and the resultant increased scrutiny of bean counters, a working knowledge of proven practices provides a clear advantage.

Want to jump-start results? Plumb the best direct marketing books and articles (including, I cannot resist adding, the ones I have written), websites, e-letters, and trade journals. Seek out and listen to the industry's seasoned pros. Priceless information awaits, ready for you to capitalize on it.

Knowing what's inside the box puts you in a position to better work outside of it—responsibly. In turn, you'll have an opportunity to add discoveries of your own to an ever-growing repository of useful knowledge. Who knows? Tomorrow's marketing giants may someday stand on your shoulders.

Part Seven

Myth and Reality

Chapter 39

Despite What You Heard, It Ain't the Sizzle that Sells

Here's a nugget of advertising wisdom that isn't: "It's not the steak that sells, it's the sizzle." Tired cliché aside, it is meaningless at best and untrue at worst.

Low-quality steaks sizzle just like high-quality ones. So do wet sponges. I hope that grill noises wouldn't seduce you into paying as much for a Denny's steak or a freshly grilled sponge as you would for a Morton's or Ruth's Chris steak. It is not the sizzle but consistent delivery on a brand promise that sells.

To be fair, *sizzle* in this case is intended as a metaphor. It refers to *hot* advertising. Since *hot* is no more easily defined than *sizzle,* the distinction isn't of much help. Nor does it help that one person's *hot* or *sizzle* is another's *meh.*

Moreover, advertising history has plenty of presumed hot campaigns that flopped and tepid or outright frigid ones that flew. *Sizzle* isn't just an elusive standard. It's a useless one.

Some people hold off bestowing sizzle status until after a campaign has run its course. If the campaign becomes popular and sales go up, they invoke sizzle. This is great if you like circular reasoning.

Instead of aspiring to sizzle, you might aspire to relevance and see what happens.

Chapter 40

More Creative Than Thou

A near-sacred myth holds that when advertising is truly creative, sales inevitably follow. I call it the Creativity Myth, and it has four effects, all of them unfortunate:

1. Clients waste money giving agencies more incentive to out-creative one another than to build sales.

2. Creative people prematurely and unwisely dismiss the tried-and-proven.

3. Some creative people develop an annoying, more-creative-than-thou attitude.

4. Those of us who create measurable advertising often end up the subject of ridicule. (Cue disdainful voice: *"Click here to order now.* How original.")

The myth grew to prominence during the Creative Revolution of the 1960s. This was the era of daring campaigns for Volkswagen, Avis, Clairol, Benson & Hedges, and others. Sales of these products soared. And, for the first time, advertising became popular.

Advertisers leapt to the conclusion that creativity was all it took to rocket a product to success. It was a classic display of *selection bias*, the often unconscious tendency to cherry-pick data that support preexisting beliefs and overlook data that do not. Selection bias can sneak up on anyone. Maternity ward employees commonly avow that more births occur under a full moon. In reality, they fail to note the sky on other busy nights. Likewise, had the new champions of creativity bothered to count creative campaigns that failed or mundane ones that succeeded, they would have understood that creativity, far from being the one crucial ingredient, is but one of many.

The misconception endures, often accompanied by the *post hoc ergo propter hoc* fallacy, the assumption that what happened first caused what happened next. "We ran the ads and sales went up. What more do you need?" Well, a lot more. Despite a glut of New Age books that claim otherwise, coincidences happen. If you don't believe me, I suggest a visit to *http://tylervigen.com/spurious-correlations*. There you will discover a host of remarkable coincidences, unless you believe that the number of films in which Nicholas Cage stars truly is a reliable predictor of the number of people who drown in swimming pools.

Some people defend the Creativity Myth this way: "A campaign that flopped wasn't truly creative." That's like proving that all cows are white with back spots by dismissing brown cows as not truly bovine. Readers who are into logical fallacies will see in this the No True Scotsman Fallacy.

Don't waste your time trying to convince Creativity Myth devotees. They are not likely to care. But *you* should care. Having dispatched the myth for yourself, you're in a great position to profit from a rational approach to creativity. When you do, two vital facts emerge:

1. Creativity is a powerful tool, but ...

2. Creativity alone cannot carry the load.

Creativity can mean a wild new approach. V8 Vegetable Juice sales shot up when they scrapped advertising the product as delicious and refreshing—I mean, have you tasted the stuff?—and touted it as an easy way to eat your vegetables.

But creativity can be equally manifest in an ingenious nuance. In his book *Tested Advertising Methods*, legendary measurable advertising champion John Caples told of how changing one word boosted sales. His headline "How to Fix Cars" outsold his earlier version, "How to Repair Cars," by 20 percent. The not-for-profit organization SETI (Search for Extraterrestrial Intelligence), founded by Carl Sagan, experienced a 73 percent increase in direct mail response when it switched from a black to a white envelope. I can't speak for you, but I think Caples's and SETI's solutions, though tiny, were highly creative.

Your creative breakthrough may be a dramatic new approach à la V8 or a subtle word change à la Caples. You may or may not win an advertising award, but you will win big on the balance sheet.

As for the more-creative-than-thou crowd, unless impressing them is listed as one of your marketing objectives, I recommend not worrying about what they think.

Chapter 41

The "Avoid the Appearance of Selling" Myth

Everyone knows that lemmings commit mass suicide by drowning, one side of our moon is always dark, and sugar makes kids hyper. Likewise, every marketer knows that people won't buy if they can tell you're trying to sell them something.

Beware what everyone knows. The above "facts" are all false. I'll leave it to you to follow up on lemmings, the moon, and sugar. Right now, let's debunk that silly myth about the need to avoid looking like you're trying to sell something when you're trying to sell something.

Imagine two salespeople, both presentable and charming. Salesperson A shows up at your door, engages you in conversation, mentions the product, and avoids directly stating a purpose for the visit. Salesperson B shows up at your door, states the purpose of his or her visit, identifies problems and shows how the product solves them, and encourages you to buy. Now imagine that you're a sales manager. Which one would you hire?

If that thought experiment hasn't convinced you to hire (and to run marketing campaigns that resemble) Salesperson B, let's move on to hard evidence.

Quick—what's the most common thing that successful salespeople do that unsuccessful ones fail to do?

If you said "ask for the sale" or, in larger transactions, "advance the sale," give yourself a point. You'll never hear successful salespeople worry about letting it be known that a sale is afoot. You will frequently hear it from unsuccessful ones. Good marketing should do what good salespeople do.

Quick—which one, a direct response or a brand marketer, is more likely to know what kind of advertising produces the most sales?

If you chose the direct marketer, give yourself another point. Brand marketers generally infer campaign results from indirect data, but they rarely can quantify them. Direct marketers don't have to infer. The very nature of direct response ensures knowing what's working, when, and by how much. While you may hear a brand marketer eschew overt selling, you'll never hear it from an experienced direct marketer. Indeed, ongoing direct response tests continue to show that the time-honored techniques of clearly showcased benefits, compelling incentives, and urging action still work, and work best.

Besides, get real. Do you really think your subtlety is fooling anyone? The moment anyone visits your website or store, watches or hears your commercial, or reads your ad, email, or direct mail, it is tacitly understood that you are selling. No one will be shocked to learn that a sale is afoot.

Why do so many marketers believe that people won't buy if you overtly sell? Besides, that is, that some marketers are morons. One reason may be that people often equate selling with pressuring or badgering. They needn't. Selling is the process of meeting wants and needs with products or services. You can add pressuring and badgering if you like, though I don't recommend it and it certainly isn't a requirement.

Perhaps it's simply that the notion has been around for a long time. As with tales of lemmings, moons, and sugar, it's natural not to question commonly held beliefs.

Or perhaps it's because this particular myth is a comfortable one. Most creative people don't go into advertising because they are eager to sell. They go into advertising because it's damned difficult to make a living pursuing their first love, namely, the arts. Can't break into the movie industry? Make commercials. Can't get a novel published? Write ads. Can't make a living as a fine artist? Go into commercial art. Such do not consider themselves salespeople. It is their art that matters. Thanks to the Avoid the Appearance of Selling Myth, along with the equally convenient Sales Magically Come from Great Creativity Myth, creative people can dwell peacefully within their comfort zone.

To deny that marketing is about selling is to embrace and promote a costly myth. The current economic environment is no place for it. If your marketing department or agency embraces the myth, it's time to stop theorizing and learn at the feet of real salespeople.

Chapter 42

The P.T. Barnum Myth

A well-known axiom attributed to Phineas Taylor Barnum states, "All publicity is good publicity." Marketing hangs a good part of its hat on the metrics of reach, rating points, and awareness, which makes it tempting to take the assertion at face value and use it to validate marketing geared only to help clients "get noticed."

Never mind that there is no record of Barnum's having said it. Marketers should be more concerned with the fact that it simply isn't true.

It's possible to cherry-pick data to make all publicity appear positive. A Bartles & Jaymes wine cooler campaign featured a pair of awkward, lovable fuddy-duddies who said nothing about the product—in fact, one of them never spoke—and sales skyrocketed. Lady Gaga profited from rampant speculation about her keeping one eye hidden from cameras. Sales of Etch A Sketch reportedly increased when a staffer likened it to presidential hopeful Mitt Romney.

But cherry-picking proves nothing beyond a penchant for selection bias. Pulling only yellow gumdrops from a package hardly establishes that all gumdrops are yellow.

Reverse cherry-picking, on the other hand, can be useful for *disproving*. A single discovery of black swans in 1697 by

Willem de Laming was all it took to permanently debunk the centuries-old conviction that swans came only in white.

We can equally resort to reverse cherry-picking to dispatch the claim that all publicity is good. The career of former South Carolina Governor Mark Sanford tanked as fast as publicity rose of his alleged hike of the Appalachian Trail. Intense media coverage of Mel Gibson's hateful epithets sabotaged his theretofore-unassailable career. Abundant late night comedy show references did not spur sales of the Yugo automobile. And Kodak, arguably the world's most-known name in cameras and film, filed for bankruptcy.

It's easy to cite factors, publicity aside, that contributed or led to each demise. That is exactly the point. For publicity to be good, it needs something positive to work with.

Beware the marketer who promises to "get your name out there." Bernie Madoff got his name out there, too.

If "getting your name out there" was all it took to be a successful marketer, this and all other books about marketing would comprise but one sentence: "Make lots of noise."

Chapter 43

The Four-Letter Word Myth

Tender ears beware. In this chapter I repeatedly use the four-letter word *sell*, along with the related words *sales* and *selling*. My apologies if you are offended, or if impressionable children happen to look over your shoulder and see the offending words. It's just that I think it's high time we stood up for the above-referenced S-words and wore them like a badge of honor.

You have my friend Brent to thank for this diatribe. One day he arrived at the office peeved because, the evening before, a neighbor had suggested that someone who sold cars "worked in marketing." Brent, you see, did market research. *That*, he would tell you, was real marketing. Salespeople just sell stuff, which was quite beneath him.

I didn't do a very good job of applying balm to his poor, bruised ego. I told him that any alleged marketer who looked down on selling and thought that selling wasn't marketing needed a stern lecture, a lesson in humility, a dictionary, and maybe even a spanking.

You may not be a salesperson. Your job may not put you face-to-face with customers. You may be way off in an office, busily strategizing, programming, creative-directing, writing, designing, production-managing, web-designing, data-manipulating, researching, tabulating, account-executing, or what-have-you-ing. But the person on the sales floor, *whose job is to finish the process that all of your behind-the-scenes marketing work exists to set up*, that person most certainly "works in marketing." And *you* most certainly are in the business of selling.

Marketers bend over backward to avoid using the S-words. But let's be honest. The ultimate goal of marketing is to get people to buy stuff, and the word most English speakers use for "getting people to buy stuff" is "selling."

There's no need to be abashed about being in the selling business. If you must use a euphemism, I suppose there's no harm in it *as long as you don't slip into denial*. Failing to concede that marketing is selling risks mistaking the execution for the goal. Prose that makes an English professor proud and design that's the envy of the art community but fail to sell are not marketing. If we don't acknowledge that, we are not marketers.

I wasn't joking about wearing the S-word like a "badge of honor." Responsible, customer-oriented selling makes an economy thrive, and making an economy thrive makes a society thrive. Any economist will tell you that a sure way to help the world out of a recession and promote long-term prosperity is to put money in circulation. Money circulates only when people buy. And people buy only when people sell.

Which means that when you admit to selling, you can admit to it with pride.

These days not just people tucked away in marketing departments avoid use of the S-word. Even salespeople have begun to eschew it. Clothing salesperson? Bite your tongue. That high school student working part time for minimum wage in that trendy mall store is a *personal fashion consultant*. "How impressive," one cannot help but yawn.

Chances are that S-word avoidance has something to do with stereotypes of loud dressers and pushy personalities. I'm not going to say that those stereotypes have no basis in fact. Rather, I'm going to make a distinction between *selling* and *hustling*. I am all for selling, and wholly against hustling. Responsible, customer-oriented selling doesn't consist of pushing or in any way taking unfair advantage. It consists of presenting relevant products and services and persuading with solid benefits.

What you call your profession is your business. But let's proudly own selling as the point of what we do, and allow it to drive our work. And let's remind those who take umbrage at our language that responsible selling as described above is needful and socially beneficial.

Part Eight

How Not to Do Research Like an Utter Fool

Chapter 44

A Research Lesson from the Restroom

The information about brain hemispheres is correct, however, the notion of creative people as "right brained" and analytical people as "left brained" is a myth.

There is a right and a wrong way to predict customer behavior. To illustrate, I shall invite you to accompany me to the office restroom.

But first, circulate a survey asking people if they wash before leaving said facilities. Make sure they know they're answering with complete anonymity, or 100 percent will answer in the affirmative.

OK, time to visit the restroom.

Choose a stall from which you can tell, without recognizing individuals, when people wash. Hang an "out of order" sign on the outside and then hide inside with the door closed. Now, count.

If your results are typical, between 60 and 80 percent of survey respondents will say they wash, but only about 10 to 20 percent actually will when they think no one is watching. If you work in my office building, don't ask how I know.

This exercise tells us something important about research. Namely, that even in anonymous surveys, asking people to explain or predict their behavior is pointless. Some people lie, but more often people simply haven't a clue about what they do, much less would do, much less why.

This may surprise marketers, but not brain surgeons. When human brain hemispheres are surgically separated, you can communicate with one side of the brain while the other side remains oblivious. Tell a split-brain patient via the right brain to walk, and the patient will comply. Then ask the patient via the left brain, "Why are you walking?" The only truthful answer is "I don't know," but left brains don't admit to not knowing. The left brain will make up an answer from whole cloth, like "I want to get a drink of water" or "I'm checking out a noise I heard in the hall," and the patient will utter it and mean it.

In *The Blank Slate: The Modern Denial of Human Nature*, author and Harvard University psychology head Steven Pinker explains:

> "We have no reason to think that the baloney-generator in the patient's left hemisphere is behaving any differently from ours as we make sense of the inclinations emanating from the rest of our brains. The conscious mind … is a spin doctor."

So the wrong way to predict the success of a marketing campaign is to ask people in focus groups or phone surveys how they think they'll react to it. The right way is to find the marketer's equivalent of a restroom stall, hide inside, and take notes.

Here's an example. We created two TV spots for a software client. Everyone had guesses as to which would work better, but knowing what opinions are worth, we ran both spots on an alternating schedule. While they ran, we hid in a metaphorical restroom stall, that is, we hid in our offices, and counted calls for a month.

We found that for one of the spots, every five dollars spent on airtime returned a dollar in revenue. Math isn't my strong suit, but I didn't need a calculator to figure out that persisting in trading five dollars for one would bankrupt my client fast.

Happily, we only had to spend 29 cents airing the other spot to earn a dollar in revenue. Our client took that spot, invested $29,000 airing it, and earned a return of $100,000. That's a $71,000 gross profit. I figured that out without a calculator, too.

Asking people which offer or spot they liked better would not have yielded reliable data. That emerged only when we created a real situation and watched unobserved.

The late John Wanamaker famously lamented, "I know that half of what I spend on advertising is wasted; I only wish I knew which half." Good news, marketers. With a little imagination and restraint, and without spending a bundle, you can prune the losers and identify the winners early. You can avoid wasting that elusive half in the first place.

Chapter 45

Direct Response as a Research Tool

Besides the fact that I don't like cocktails, you may want to think twice before inviting me to your next cocktail party. Since a customary ice-breaker is to feign interest in what the person you just met does for a living, you would place each of your guests at risk of having to hear me rhapsodize, ad infinitum, about the virtues of direct response marketing as a sales tool.

But this time I'm going to rhapsodize about another, lesser-known way to profit from direct response. Besides being useful for selling goods and services, it is a powerful tool for peering deep inside the mind of a customer.

Direct response marketing as consumer research

• *Predictive research.* Too often, researchers assume that asking people questions is a good way to find out how they'll act. Nonsense. People cannot predict how they'll react to your marketing. Unfortunately, that doesn't keep them from giving you their best guess and meaning it. Well-meaning respondents assured researchers that they would buy *Cosmopolitan* magazine brand yogurt, Colgate brand frozen meals, Bic disposable underwear, McDonald's brand children's clothing, and Vicks brand aspirin. Each of these products flopped.

Moreover, human behavior changes when people know someone is watching. If you don't believe me, consider any personal habit you indulge privately that you wouldn't indulge publicly. If you don't want to own up to one, consider the habits of someone you don't like.

As a research tool, direct response eliminates both problems. Respondents don't try to predict their behavior; they simply act, blissfully unaware that anyone is keeping track. Results are tallied from afar, so no one is influenced by the idea that someone is "watching."

• *Defining a point-of-purchase strategy.* For years, *Reader's Digest* depended on point-of-purchase sales driven only by the table of contents on its cover. It always featured a few titles in large type at the top. Determining *which* titles to feature was crucial to point-of-purchase sales. How did they know which titles to showcase? They ran small newspaper ads offering to send respondents three articles, free, from a list of 20. Once they knew which were the three most-requested articles, they featured them on the next cover.

• *Testing brand strength.* A large, well-known national brand acquired one of my agency's clients, a smaller but still well-known national brand in its own right. A debate soon arose as to whether the smaller brand should retain its identity or take on that of the parent company.

We divided a representative sample of the market into three groups. Over a few months, we mailed each group a series of offers. For one group, we featured the larger company's brand. For another, we featured the smaller company's brand. The remaining group showed only the brand of a local dealer. All of the offers were identical.

When we counted responses, we found that *the brand made no difference whatsoever*. Changing the offer, however, made a huge difference. Both sides of the debate had to face the sobering possibility that their brand wasn't as powerful as they'd supposed, and that extending the right free offer mattered more than who extended it.

This was not a test of brand power in general. But if you dare, a test like this can provide a valuable reality check.

• *Most compelling claim.* The legendary John Caples was working on a newspaper campaign to promote a food product. He narrowed his choices to two overall claims: one centered on providing good nutrition for the family, while the other centered on receiving praise for serving a tasty meal. Moms were the target in those days, and in focus groups they overwhelmingly endorsed the nutrition theme. Ever wary, Caples ran a split-copy test in several newspapers. The promise of praise for a tasty meal produced far more orders. Caples dumped the nutrition idea and successfully rolled out a campaign based on winning praise.

Even if—heaven forbid—direct response marketing doesn't figure into your regular media plan, perhaps you should make room for it in your research plan. In many cases, you can use direct response marketing far more effectively, for far less cost, than other research methods to plumb non-direct-response questions.

It really is that simple. Therefore, expect your research firm to say it isn't. At cocktail parties, people who work for research firms avoid me the most.

Chapter 46

Data Sans Wiggle-Room

stute marketers may have noticed that the first word in the term "direct response marketing" happens to be "direct." It is apt in more than one sense. Direct marketers advertise *directly* to carefully selected targets, and those targets respond *directly* back in return.

But direct marketing offers another, valuable variety of directness not to be overlooked: data without wiggle-room. It is ideal for marketers who are less interested in defending their latest effort and more interested in finding out whether and how well the latest effort performed.

Traditional mass media campaigns tend to be *in*direct. Customers respond over time via a third party such as a store or website. Between receipt of an awareness message and action taken at a store, other factors such as politics, breaking news, the recession, or retailers' practices can come into play. Therein lies the wiggle-room. When sales rise, it is natural and tempting and may even appear reasonable to credit the latest ad campaign. When sales disappoint, it is convenient to invoke "other factors" and credit the campaign with having kept things from getting worse. And why not? In the absence of direct, causal data, one inference is as good as another.

No wonder the late Scots poet and novelist Andrew Lang famously lamented, "An unsophisticated forecaster uses statistics as a drunken man uses lampposts—for support rather than for illumination."

On the other hand, there is no evidence that Lang used direct response marketing. Had he done so, he might have taken delight in its uncanny ability to illuminate.

While direct response can be and is effectively used to drive shoppers to third parties, it also stands as the original interactive, measurable advertising practice. It allows marketers to control for outside factors in order to arrive at direct, causal data. With a properly planned and executed program, there is no need for inference. You can know what works and what doesn't, and the extent to which outside factors do and don't affect results.

Direct response marketing tends to attract marketers who are eager to give a project their best and know rather than guess at results. For brave marketers more interested in illumination than support, there is no better lamppost.

Part Nine

Direct Mail In An Online World

Chapter 47

Of Mail and Monitor

The publisher of a respected advertising magazine called me. The president of her bank had sent her a personal note, just to check up and make sure the bank was treating her well. Since the bank was my client, she thought I'd like to know. Wasn't that cool of the bank president?

I hated telling her, but thousands of the bank's highest-balance customers received that letter. I should know. I wrote it, and my agency mailed it.

Actually, I loved telling her. I positively gloated. But after shoving my ego back under the veneer of feigned humility where I usually and not very successfully try to hide it, I realized something. Thanks—ironically—to email and the Internet, direct mail may now pack a mightier punch.

Time for a disclaimer. Please don't write to me defending email marketing. I'm not attacking it. I shall contrast it with direct mail only to bring out some of the latter's advantages. Email has advantages, too, but that's another topic for another day.

A number of unique factors work in direct mail's favor. One is what your English literature teacher called "willing suspension of disbelief"—our ability to set aside reality and lose ourselves in a story. When a direct mail letter shows up in a personally addressed, stamped envelope, part of us wants to believe that someone took a moment to compose, print, address and post it, just for us. All the better if the letter calls us by name and bears a signature in fountain pen-evoking blue. There simply is no electronic substitute.

Willing suspension of disbelief knows no demographic limitations. Consider my publisher friend. A technologically savvy marketing insider, she knows my shop, understands digital printing, publishes my articles, and on occasion pops for lunch. Had she paused to analyze, she would easily have seen that the letter in her hand was direct mail. But—and this is the point—she chose not to pause and analyze. Nor did other recipients. You'll recall that these were high-balance customers, not exactly the intellectual dregs of society. Of those who replied, 80 percent willingly suspended their disbelief and thanked the bank president for writing.

Whether or not your direct mail includes an envelope or sales letter, it appears that the public would rather receive advertising mail in a mailbox than on a computer. Higher response rates provide one indicator. The near-overnight appearance of spam laws and filters provides another. No sooner had email blasts arrived than the public demanded laws restricting them, servers blocking them, and junk filters dispatching them. By contrast, laws governing physical mail are far less restrictive, despite more than 200 years of opportunity to enact them. You may have noticed there is no junk file into which Standard-Rate mail disappears, nor must you worry about an intermediary blacklisting you. The public simply doesn't demand it.

Besides reflecting a market preference, the absence of such controls offers a practical advantage. Everyone must look through their physical mail in order to decide what to read and what to chuck. Not so with email. There, one click on a Junk or Spam icon dooms a marketer to oblivion.

Let's not overlook that people have always looked forward to getting their mail, and still do. Most people can tell you what time their mail arrives. Most bring it in daily and eagerly dig through it. News flash: They're not hoping to find bills. They're hoping to find letters and, believe it or not, relevant advertising mail.

I suspect it is for these reasons that our shop and others find that intelligent, well-targeted direct mail continues to perform well. But note my use of qualifiers like *relevant, intelligent*, and *well-targeted*.

Email and other online media are useful and powerful in their own right. But when planning a direct response media mix, it's important to remember that there are some things a mailbox can deliver that a monitor just can't.

Chapter 48

Fun with Lumpy Mail

There's nothing quite like a box or bulging padded envelope in the mail. It makes your inner child hop up and down, tug your sleeve and ask, nay, nag: "What's inside? Huh? HUH? WHAT'S INSIDE?" This happens even when you know what's inside because it was you who ordered the package.

That eager inner child dwells within us all. Even hard-to-reach corporate curmudgeons, who take pride in chucking direct mail unopened, or delegating the task to administrative assistants, harbor such a child. And that is precisely why well-executed lumpy mail works. It has the uncanny ability to find its way to the curmudgeon's hands and, very often, heart. It even charms their administrative assistants, some of whom, rumor has it, also once had hearts.

If you want to reach business decision-makers, lumpy mail is your secret weapon. I suppose I could use the more common term, "three-dimensional direct mail," but my inner child likes saying "lumpy."

How powerful is lumpy mail? Consider a credit card provider seeking face-to-face meetings with financial institution CEOs. Our agency mailed each CEO a box containing a sales letter and a First Class Business Reply card. I should also mention that the box was five feet long to accommodate the pair of stilts that we enclosed. The sales letter promised to help banks compete with "the big guys." Our client set appointments with 40 percent of the mailing list and booked over $65 million in business the first year alone.

Not that lumpy mail must be as elaborate or costly as sending a pair of stilts. For a client with a tiny budget, we enclosed a fake mustache—for less than a dollar apiece—with a letter and reply card in a Number 10 envelope. The envelope headline read, "Clever disguise enclosed." The pitch? That retailing our client's product would be immensely profitable. The mustache? To hide from long-lost friends showing up for a handout. It pulled a 25 percent response.

Then there was the air horn we mailed for a community bank (36 percent response), the kazoo for a business service (25 percent), the Lone Ranger mask for a half million-dollar software product (25 percent), the beanbag elephant for a regional bank (56 percent), and the two-headed coin for a transit company (47 percent).

I'll resist the temptation to keep raving. Let's move on to what makes lumpy mail work from a strategic standpoint. Here are six musts:

1. Send something of value. Junk doesn't impress. Neither does a pen or mug with your logo. Note that "of value" needn't mean "expensive." The mustache cost our client less than a buck. Recipients kept it because it was fun. Many donned it and paraded around the office.

2. Send something with "head-scratcher" value. The last thing you need is for recipients to know what you plan to say before you say it. Make them scratch their head and wonder, "Why did they send me a hockey puck?" (The hockey puck mailing, by the way, pulled an 8 percent response.) To find out, they will have to read.

3. Write a darned good sales letter. All that the lumpy enclosure does is charm, grab attention, and make people read. Then it's the letter's job to sell. Do not substitute or enclose a flyer. Not even a really cool one. You will drive response down.

4. Don't say too much. Tell enough to create but not to satisfy curiosity. Then invite the reader to contact you to learn more. Keep the letter to a page, and add no literature besides a reply card.

5. Be relevant. "Now that I have your attention..." isn't strategic; it's juvenile. Your lumpy enclosure must underscore a salient point. When we mailed high-end wooden puzzles to hospital-based pathologists, we likened the puzzle to laboratory management challenges. Recipients could receive the puzzle's solution by meeting with a sales rep. (15 percent response.)

6. Follow up by phone. In every case cited here resulting in meetings with more than 25 percent of recipients, the difference was telephone follow-up. Lumpy mail generates inquiries on its own, but you'll double or triple results by calling every name on the list. Try opening with, "I'm the one who sent you the life preserver." (Yes, we mailed those, too. 40 percent.) Then ask for an appointment. (Hint: Mail in smaller quantities, on which you can more realistically follow up.)

Lumpy mailings are usually quite well received, but I need to warn you about the rare stick-in-the mud who will say, "If you must do this to get my attention, you can't be any good." Should that happen, congratulations. You've just identified someone you don't want for a customer. Move on to the next name.

Lumpy mailings are powerful, effective, and a blast. Right now, we're preparing to mail deodorant soap for a high-end audio products manufacturer. Next, we're mailing volleyballs for a law firm.

I'll let you know how it goes.

Update: The volleyballs pulled a 25 percent response. The soap bombed. Can't win 'em all.

Chapter 49

The Lowly Reply Card

Eons ago when I worked on the client side, my employer's ad agency invited me for a tour. The umpteenth person who had to feign being happy to meet me was the copy chief. This fellow's ego would have fit easily inside a retail giant's main warehouse (I know, look who's talking), so the account executive who introduced us decided to needle him. The needling took the form of introducing him as "the guy who writes those reply cards in direct mail."

While they yucked it up at the intended, clever slight, I smiled inwardly at the unwitting betrayal of their lack of knowledge. "Those reply cards" do an important job, and it takes a pro to write a good one.

If you think that shouldn't be so, I'd be the first to agree. If I ruled the world, all direct mail recipients would do the following in this order: read the envelope copy, pause to bask in its brilliance, savor the sales letter, reread parts of it for sheer joy, pore over and consider framing the brochure, reverently ponder the lift letter, then and only then check YES on the reply card, and drop it in the nearest mailbox before they knew what had hit them.

I can't speak for you, but experience and tracking have shown me that I don't rule the world. Some direct mail recipients dig out and read the reply card first, most likely because they want a shortcut to knowing what the marketer is up to. When that happens, the reply card has the daunting task of single-handedly capturing their attention so that they'll read the rest of the envelope's contents.

Even more challenging are people who read all the contents of a direct mail package but have the temerity to wait for a few days before responding. Some even have the gall to discard the rest of the package and keep only the reply card. In the entirely likely event that their memory has waned by the time they pull out and reread the reply card, no sales letter, brochure, or lift letter is there to help out. The reply card must sell the product, tout the incentive offer and close the sale, all by itself.

Even when people keep the envelope and its other contents, it is the reply card that they mail back, or hold in their hand when calling or logging on to respond. Catalog marketers know that even people who purchase by phone or online may first organize their purchase by completing the order form, which is the reply card's close cousin.

The reply card deserves your full effort. What makes for a good, hard-working reply card? Here are some tips.

• **Give readers a box to check.** It will increase response. Make the box square. Do not color it or put a shadow behind it, no matter how design-y it looks. Otherwise, the box will look like a bullet, and people don't check bullets.

• **Copy should read like the reader's response to a call to action.** Like, "YES! Send me the..." or, "SURE, I accept your free trial offer for a..." It may seem redundant, since a check mark and a mailed card imply a "yes," but putting it in type increases response.

• **Summarize main selling points,** benefits, the incentive offer, expiration date and reassurances like "no obligation," guarantees, return policies, and so on. It goes without saying that you'll need to do this with very few words. Set aside plenty of time for the task. Concision to this degree isn't easy.

• **Clarity sells better than cleverness.**

• **Make your phone number and your URL too big to miss.** If your art director doesn't object, it's probably too small.

• **Don't print the reply card on coated stock.** People need to be able to write on it.

• **Study and emulate reply cards created by direct mail pros.**

• **If the reply card is to be sent back in the mail without an envelope, run it by the U.S. Postal Service** to ensure it meets their standards.

Reply cards may not look like much, but they are powerful and crucial selling tools. If you're ever introduced as the person who writes them, blush and say, "Aw, shucks."

Chapter 50

Think Inside the Box

As one who is all for instant gratification, I love the Internet. I can preview anything on-the-spot. If I like the preview, I can download the real thing and revel in it then and there.

Provided, that is, that I never want to download anything besides pictures, video, sound, or text. A non-media product—say, that new deodorant my friends are so eager for me to try—is another matter. Outside of sci-fi movies, not even the best 3-D printer can download a 3.5-ounce container of deodorant. Nor will sniffing the monitor or rubbing it in your underarm produce the desired result. Never mind how I know.

Don't despair. There is a way to download non-media products at home. With apologies to self-help gurus, this is one time to think inside the box. More specifically, inside the mailbox.

Not long ago, a sport jacket called out to me from the Lands' End website. By some miracle, I had lived to that point without it. Yet I hesitated. I couldn't quite judge the fabric quality from the photo. Nor was I sure about the color, for, as anyone who goes on press-checks knows, monitors know no universal color code. Fortunately, someone smart at Lands' End had placed a "Request swatch" button next to the product photo. Request swatch I did, and the merchant promptly downloaded the swatch to my mailbox. The day it arrived, I ordered the rest of the sport jacket, which was downloaded to my mailbox a few days later.

So here's a thought. If your marketing strategy depends on letting people kick metaphorical tires before making a purchase, maybe you should offer to download a bit of tire to their mailbox.

Back to that deodorant. You know what the ubiquitous "They" say about old habits. You'll have a hard time getting brand-loyal people to entrust the well-being of their armpits to a new brand, no matter how free from underarm angst the sexy people in your ads appear. But if your brand is superior enough to win them over with a trial, downloading samples to carefully selected mailboxes might just change those old habits, plus spur word of mouth.

Tracking and cost accounting are important. Distributing samples is about creating customers, not about creating impressions. Include a coupon with each sample. Though not all converted customers will use the coupon, you can extrapolate from those who do.

Part Ten

Tales of Terror
from the Trenches

Chapter 51

Misadventures in Marketing

Direct marketers can be an arrogant lot. As one myself, I should know. We crow about our rules, disdain those who don't embrace them, brag about a mega percent response—and conveniently ignore work that bombed.

But I'm going to let in you in a little secret. We really don't know everything. We just love acting like we do. So, for a change, I thought I'd get off my high horse and, instead of trying to convince you that DM is nirvana, share some misadventures from our industry.

Crushing results

In 2001, a Midwest catalog marketer enclosed unwrapped dinner mints in a mass mailing. The mints were crushed to white powder in the mail. That wasn't the bad part. The bad part was that while they were in transit, the Anthrax scare hit the fan. The mailing drew quite the response. From the FBI.

"Sorry to hear you died"

A woman wrote to a hospital CEO to complain that her father, who had died months earlier in that very hospital, was still on their mailing list. The CEO sent a letter of apology, which would have been fine if he hadn't sent it to her father.

Poor targeting

When direct mail fails, the Number One reason is poor targeting. Take the contact lens offer that came to my home, addressed to Sebastian Cuno. There was a Sebastian in my household at the time. He was the family cat. He expressed no interest in contact lenses.

Chivalry is dead

Not long after forger and pipe-bomber Mark Hoffman went to jail, a competing Utah agency mailed packages about the size of a briefcase. Executives on the receiving end were understandably reluctant to open them. A few did the honorable thing: They asked a secretary to open the package in another room.

Bad phone

Transposed phone numbers are doubly embarrassing when your objective is to generate phone inquiries. I know of a financial institution (no, I'm not going to tell you which one) whose ad agency (no, it wasn't us, but so what? Our turn will come*) transposed two digits in an 800 number. The result happened to be a porn line.

Toward a bran image

For a medical clinic's grand opening, we offered free ice cream gift certificates. It worked. The clinic was overrun with visitors. But an indignant attorney wrote: "I am shocked that a health care organization would encourage people to ingest ice cream." I was horrified. I mean, who knew they were *ingesting* the stuff? The attorney suggested offering bran muffins instead. The ice cream offer performed beyond expectation. I doubt that bran muffins would have been successful, although they would certainly have changed the outcome, so to speak.

"We aim to bore"

A client asked us to rewrite a direct response ad we created for him. "It has personality," he said, "and that's just not us."

Murphy at work

No mailing list is 100 percent accurate. So, when a large client wanted to know why the fussiest member of their board of directors received three of the same mailing at his home on the same day, there could be only one answer: Because these mistakes must happen, and the fussiest director is the last person you want it to happen to.

---

*Actually, our turn did come. We misprinted a phone number for a major client of our own. Luckily, the resultant number was available, and our quick-thinking client grabbed it.

Chapter 52

The Day Silo Regretted Waxing Colloquial

I'm all for lightening up and writing copy with a conversational tone, but sometimes it backfires.

Take, for instance, the time Silo thought it would be cute to substitute a colloquialism for "dollars." Of myriad possibilities, they settled on "bananas." So it was that television viewers in selected markets learned that for a limited time Silo would sell them a stereo system for the low price of "299 bananas."

I bet you already guessed what happened next. Lots of people showed up with 299 bananas in hand. At the time, 299 bananas went for about $60. Silo wisely accepted them as payment at considerable loss.

Their next problem was what to do with all the bananas. At the end of the sale they had about 11,000 of them, more than local zoos or food banks were prepared to take.

There was a silver lining. The national press picked up the story, giving Silo positive exposure worth millions of dollars.

At least bananas smell sweet. Think what would have happened if Silo had offered the stereo for 299 clams.

Chapter 53

Readers Share Their Favorite ~~Tpyos~~ Typos

You know the log you wanted to crawl under after that typo? Stand proudly atop it instead, for you are in good company. I invited marketers worldwide to share their embarrassments. The resultant outpouring of entertaining, unpretentious tales made choosing from among them a challenge. Here are the tales, names omitted, typos (ironically) corrected, and regrettably pared for space (but without annoying ellipses).

* * *

Years ago a pharmaceutical company analyst related some of their problems. Salespeople were putting comments in the address rather than the notes field. A mailing yielded two very angry responses from separate medical groups. One received a mailing addressed to Dr. John Doe, "The Dead Guy." Another received one to Ms. Mary Smith, "The one with the big butt." Needless to say they were not getting business from those medical groups.

* * *

We were printing and inserting a credit card statement for a financial services provider. We were not responsible for the creative. Let's just say the toll free number had our customer service line ringing because a switch of a digit changed the line into a rather racy one of a sexual nature.

* * *

Wrong list was used and one personalization (my favorite) was "Dear Mrs. Mother Superior." The magazine was not all that pleased.

* * *

In the 1980s the company I worked for was printing materials for an evangelical minister. One mailing gave directions to their church in Harlem with, "go down two blocks and turn left." The word blocks was misspelled blacks. They discovered the typo on the proof, but told us to print it anyway.

* * *

Thirty years ago we did a mailing to "high-ups" but didn't realize there were problems with the software that translated honorifics into a salutation. One R.A. (Member of the Royal Academy) was [addressed as] a Rear Admiral. He wrote the chairman asking for back pension for his newly exalted status as he had only been an ordinary seaman. Said chairman was not amused.

* * *

[A publication in Wales] was to carry an ad [for a gas utility] but the copy had not reached them. The enterprising souls printed the words "this space reserved for Wales Gas." It got more applications than an ad containing every detail under the sun. The English like a challenge.

* * *

Seven million pieces headed for the recycle bins. The offer was supposed to read "you and your spouse." Instead it read "you and your souse." Guess you had to be married to a drunk to qualify.

* * *

I worked on a mailing to doctors. In the 70s we put punches in reply cards to look official. The punch took out the ni in organism. Responses were off the charts.

* * *

A large cosmetics firm developed a mailer for a skin care product. The tagline was "Ten years younger? You be the judge!" We did the piece in 18 languages. The problem? Seems the words "judge" and "suicide" are much alike in Norwegian. The Norway mailer read: "Ten years younger? Go kill yourself!" I think we sold ten bottles in Norway. Did well everywhere else, so it's pretty clear what impact that "typo" had.

* * *

A loyalty mailing went out with a typo in the phone number. The [resultant] phone number was for a porn line. [The company] worked hard to get the number, but the porn line owner didn't want to lose "loyal" customers. So for about a month, [callers] heard, "For [the rewards program], press 1. If you are ready to get naked, press 2."

Chapter 54

"That's Not All You Won't Like About Me"

Responding to our proposal, the marketing director of a company that had just retained us emailed me the not-unusual reaction, "Our CEO doesn't think anyone will read a two-page letter."

I wasn't feeling terribly tactful that day, which is to say I was feeling like my usual self, so here is what I wrote back:

> I understand the leap of faith I ask clients to make when it comes to long copy. Your CEO is not the first in my 30-year career to express doubt about it. I would have a much easier time selling our services if I made everything short. And, it would be easier to write. The trouble is this darned fiduciary responsibility I have to give you my best advice.
>
> The rule for direct mail copy length is: make it long enough to make the sale, that is, no longer and also no shorter. Number of pages is not the objective; making the sale is. Unless you're doing a "dimensional" mailing, one page is rarely enough.
>
> We recommend long copy not because we like it better but because it sells more. The direct marketing industry didn't learn this by surveying people and asking them what they'd be more likely to read; they learned it by testing it both ways and comparing the results. That's

how it came to be that a direct response axiom is, "the more you tell, the more you sell," and that is why the industry standard is long sales letters, long ads, and long commercials. People love to complain about them, but they work. The only ad agencies that say people won't read long copy are the ones that don't test and measure, or who don't know how to write long copy that holds and persuades a reader. Provided it's done right, long copy performs best.

Speaking of "provided it's done right," if your boss is concerned about a long sales letter, you should also prepare him for angst over the fact that the sales letter will indeed be a sales letter. It won't sound like him. It will use an informal tone, push benefits, use contractions, speak in first-person singular, address itself to "you," have a P.S., cover main selling points more than once, also cover main selling points more than once ... use ellipses ... use small, punchy words like "punchy" instead of big, esoteric words like "esoteric"—use dashes—and feature strong calls to action. We may use a preposition to end a sentence with. Might use fragments, too.

For an example you're sure not to like, consider the four-page sales letter we wrote for Westminster College. They had their doubts about its tone and length. It was so successful they re-used it over and over. Or consider the two-page fund raising letter we wrote for a not-for-profit organization. Also very successful.

The decision to purchase your product is a big one. Before taking action, a serious candidate will want thorough information. If you fail to supply it, you will lose sales.

> *We know what we're doing. But I don't want to push some-*
> *thing your CEO can't get 100% behind. Please don't hire*
> *us for our expertise and then not let us use it. It would be*
> *better not to proceed.*

I waited for the marketing director to send us packing with the CEO's encouragement. To my amazement, the CEO conceded that I was right and retained us.

I might add that the CEO and his entourage read my entire email. It was 487 words long.

Chapter 55

The Fine Art of Landing on Your Feet

Were it not for ill fortune, the article that became this chapter would not have been written. *Deliver,* the marketing magazine that asked me to write it, had originally planned to run a piece by somebody else.

It was a great piece, the planned one, about a restaurant chain's hot new marketing program. There was only one problem. Just before press time, the restaurant had finished testing its program, found that it failed miserably, and discontinued it. *Deliver* had no choice but to pull the article.

Fortunately, the editor always kept an extra feature article at the ready for just such an emergency.

Ha ha. Just kidding. *Deliver* was about to go to press with several vacant pages. After a brief discussion of the merits of "this space left intentionally blank" or "use this page for notes," the editors recalled an idea they'd begun developing a few weeks earlier. It was for an article about landing on one's feet in the event of the inevitable trip-up. With the editors themselves now tripped up, the idea seemed apt, even poetic. Here was a chance for the magazine not just to report on but to live the experience of picking itself up, dusting itself off, and snatching itself from the jaws of defeat.

All they needed was a pushover of an author who'd drop everything else he had going on to devote day and night to producing the new article in record time, just under the wire, saving the day, without realizing until later that he could have held out for and gotten a rush fee.

Guess who they called.

The subject of landing on one's feet requires knocking down screens and admitting that we marketers are all subject to losing our footing. To hear our myriad tales of doing the impossible to the wonder of clients and colleagues, one would think us impervious to mishap. To talk about our foibles rather than our successes is ... so ... not-us.

But sooner or later, everyone stumbles. Each of the following tales is true, either experienced first-hand or personally related to me by someone who was there. I think sharing our stumbles—and how we recover from them—can be instructive. It's helpful not to feel like the only person in the room who stumbles. It's equally helpful to realize that we can get up, rejoin the race and start winning again, often emerging stronger for the experience.

Wrong number

My friend occupied an office next to a capable, experienced direct marketer in a respected agency. He watched her eagerly open and flip through one of the catalog samples that had just arrived on her desk. This was her project, her baby.

Tens of millions of them were on their way to mailboxes all over the country. But she didn't beam. Instead, she wordlessly drew the wastebasket from under her desk and vomited into it. The phone number, throughout, was wrong.

Tens. Of. Millions.

Every marketer who has ever endured a major screw-up knows that horror. To realize that you've blown it, really blown it, in a big, irretrievable, expensive way, that the little singing orphan was wrong about the sun coming up tomorrow, the next day, or the next day after that, or possibly ever again, and that from every angle, all you see is disaster. And there's no way you'll get through it.

Yet, somehow, we do get through. Years after the fact, we may even muster a laugh as we retell the tale of that singular, send-your-stomach-crashing-through-the-floor, career-obliterating moment.

Many a comedian defines humor as "pain plus time." They may be on to something.

The rare, fortuitous outcome

Let's lighten up a bit. On rare occasions, what starts out as a mistake can end up a winner. Consider, for instance, a service company that wanted to send its most profitable clients a generous coupon. Their agency crafted a sales letter that flattered readers: They were preferred customers, no one else was receiving the coupon, and this was a token of the company's appreciation. It might have made quite the impression if the folks in the letter shop had remembered to enclose the coupon.

Chagrined, the agency apologized to the client and took full responsibility. They didn't bother blaming the letter shop. It would have been small of them, and the client could correctly have pointed out that the letter shop was under the agency's supervision. Instead, in record time and at its own expense, the agency created and mailed an envelope with the headline, "Oops!" The subhead, enclosed in parentheses, read, "Details inside." The sales letter opened with, "My mistake!" It went on to say that, this time, the coupon really was enclosed. Needless to say, the agency made sure of it.

But things were not rosy between agency and client. This was the agency's longest-standing account. The account executive's income depended on it. And at that moment, the client was displeased with the agency and skeptical of its solution. He didn't like saying "oops" to his customers. He feared it made him look incompetent. His customers counted on him to get things right. If he couldn't remember to put a piece of paper in an envelope, how could customers trust him to deliver on his promises?

In a rare twist, serendipity came to the rescue. The "Oops!" mailing produced record coupon redemptions. Now the client is considering repeating the "mistake" on purpose.

My own agency was once the beneficiary—sort of—of a profitable mistake. For a not-for-profit client selling annual memberships, we created a mailing to warn lapsed members that they were about to lose their benefits. The mailing produced the greatest number of enrollments in the client's history. But before anyone could break out the champagne, we learned that our client had inadvertently given us the wrong list. Instead of lapsed members, we had reached newly enrolled members.

Two members complained, but a surprising number simply reenrolled. Too bad there was no ethical way to roll out the program.

Not available in textbooks

Sometimes a faux pas can lead to a valuable lesson not to be found in a textbook. I once approved a campaign that included an execution with a headline in Spanish, as a service to the growing Hispanic population in our market. Not long after, I received a not-too-friendly, yet insightful, letter from an outraged consumer. Sure, our headline was in Spanish, but the body copy was in English; what good was that? Furthermore, we had used an illustration reminiscent of a stereotype, which, until she pointed it out, had been lost on this WASP. I wrote back thanking her for a lesson well learned, and meant it. I have since been vigilant in seeking to produce inclusive, equality-minded, non-stereotyping work. It's a lesson I will always appreciate.

Every marketer knows that missing deadlines is unwise. I learned the hard way that beating a deadline can be unwise, too. A client had been pressuring us to turn around a project faster than we felt was possible. Then, to our surprise, we did it. We mailed on the requested date instead of the date three days hence we'd negotiated. Strutting into the client's office expecting a hero's welcome, I nearly lost the business instead. Having taken our negotiated drop date to heart, the client had delayed informing its personnel of the promotion. I now know never to presume to please a client with a surprise early drop.

It seemed funny at the time

Perhaps the antithesis of awful moments later retold with humor would be moments that began as funny but ended up not. A highly sought-after illustrator liked to hide gags in initial roughs, but of course he always removed them from the finished product. He told me about painting a lush garden scene for a major billboard campaign. In one corner of the billboard, he couldn't resist adding two, hardly-noticeable pairs of naked feet in a compromising position poking out from under some bushes. His rough work rivaled anyone else's finished work, and this rough was no exception. The client liked the illustration as it was and approved it with no changes. The illustrator, having forgotten the feet, went happily on to his next project.

Months later, he saw the billboard—and the feet. Devastated, he called the client and apologized. If he regretted adding the feet, he regretted apologizing more. The boards had been up for weeks and no one had noticed the feet. There's no telling if the feet would have continued unnoticed, but now there was no choice: At great cost, the billboards had to come down. My friend faced the ire of his client and of the agency that had retained him. Certainly he had earned their ire, but let's be honest. Is it so hard for many of us to imagine making a similar goof?

An art director friend once mocked up a facetious ad for a hot cocoa mix. The headline said that their new French chocolate flavor was so French that it would make you "go *oui-oui.*" It was only a gag for the benefit of the client. Neither the art director nor the account executive anticipated that the client would not just love the ad, but insist on running it. They knew their client had a great sense of humor, but they didn't know it was that great.

The creative director, who hadn't seen the ad, was infuriated, but the client insisted, so the ad ran. Not knowing when to quit, the art director sent the ad to "The Tonight Show," and Jay Leno showed it during a "Headlines" segment. The client was thrilled, the creative director was not, and the art director and the account executive remained in the doghouse for months. Of course the creative director didn't for a moment consider out-and-out firing them. For one thing, they were too valuable. For another, how do you fire someone for making your client deliriously happy?

I once served a brief sentence as the advertising manager for a dour company that was embarrassed by its need to advertise, and, as I was frequently reminded, to have someone with my skill set on board at all. As you might expect, I had time on my hands. So, one day, I roughed an ad that was over-the-top inappropriate. It was for an imagined infertility product, if that tells you anything. I sent it up the ladder for approval, expecting a chuckle from my boss or perhaps from his boss. Instead, it made its way to the CEO—*who approved it*. I then had the honor of explaining to the CEO that the ad was a joke, doing my best to avoid saying that no one with taste or judgment would have approved it, and didn't he know that his company didn't even have an infertility product? I wasn't there long.

I'm falling but I can get up

Perhaps every college marketing curriculum should include "Landing on Your Feet 101." This would not be a course in glibly eluding consequences, but in embracing and learning from them.

Not even the most seasoned professional is immune to mishaps and missteps. Sometimes, as in the case of the "Oops!" mailing, a trip-up can lead to profitable discoveries. Sometimes, as in the case of running a headline in Spanish, it can lead to lessons painfully but gratefully learned.

Either way, when Fortuna calls on us to pull a rabbit from a hat, make lemonade from a lemon, or simply buck up and face consequences, surely there is solace in knowing we haven't been singled out. It can and does happen to anyone.

The trick is in emerging from the experience better than when we started into it.

Speaking of which, this piece came out better than the one about the restaurant.

Part Eleven

Real World 101

Chapter 56

Attack of the TWABS I

Not long ago, a company could launch an advertising campaign solely because an entity known as "Corporate" had set aside a budget for it. Objectives? Pishposh. As long as people remembered the ads, the board of directors and their spouses liked them, the viral video was downloaded like crazy, or the ads took top honors at an awards show, everyone assumed the campaign was working.

Alas, the good old days of ego-indulgent marketing are endangered to the point of near-extinction. This is largely due to the fact that, as undoubtedly you heard, a major recession came along at the end of 2007. Many of us are still reeling from its effects.

One result of recessions is that Those Who Allocate Budgets (TWABs) turn a skeptical eye upon all programs that consume money without being able to demonstrate a direct and clear contribution to the bottom line. This leaves traditional brand advertising particularly vulnerable. The link between recall scores, likability, downloads, and awards is at best inferred. The inference often breaks down under scrutiny. Even claims that sales increased during a campaign are not immune, for surges can result from other factors.

If you work in a branding agency, the word for this development might be "disconcerting." But if you happen to be a direct marketer or the client of one, that word should be "opportunity."

Direct response is, after all, the only form of advertising with built-in, empirical proof of its contribution to the bottom line. Good direct marketers need never resort to inferential rhetoric to justify their existence. At any given moment, they can plop under the nose of the most parsimonious TWAB a spreadsheet that shows if a direct marketing program is earning its keep, and by how much. There is no wiggle-room, no weaseling. No other advertising discipline can do that. In an economy in which every dime counts, direct response is the obsessive-compulsive, jaundiced-eyed TWAB's dream.

But, to paraphrase *Hamlet*, here's the rub. We cannot assume that every TWAB understands the advantages of direct response marketing. These days, there is a real danger that your friendly neighborhood TWAB will decide that all marketing and advertising, direct response included, is baby-less bath water. We may find ourselves summarily discarded when we really should have had our own tub.

We may be in part to blame. Half of the direct marketer's historical challenge has been to get clients to consider that maybe, just maybe, awards, popularity and recall scores are not all they're cracked up to be. Since there's nothing quite like a shortage of funds to make clients figure out such things for themselves, the economy may have taken over that fight for us. It's just as well. A study cited by the New England Skeptical Society shows that, a few weeks after the fact, most people unwitting recall a debunked myth as having been confirmed. It's possible that in trying to debunk advertising myths, we have in fact been reinforcing them.

I shudder to think. Especially since we could have put that effort into the other half of our challenge—namely, that of establishing direct response as the desirable, profitable alternative that actually works. Even here, it is ironic how often direct marketers ignore their own advice by selling the features of direct response rather than its benefits. To wit: we brag that direct response is built on tested and proven methods, yet we often stop short of saying what tested and proven methods do for the client (produce revenue); we say that direct response is accountable, but fail to drive home what that accountability demonstrates (that we're producing revenue); we say that direct response allows for ongoing adjustment and improvement, but forget to point out what ongoing adjustment and improvement do for the client (produce ever-increasing revenue).

But right now we have a renewed chance to sell direct response in glowing, positive terms. Business decision-makers know that besides cutting expenses, they must also find new ways to produce revenue. Since that is exactly what direct response marketing does, this is our opportunity. It's not too late to seize it by doing a more effective job of standing up for direct response marketing. And since the economy has largely relieved us of having to point out the drawbacks of traditional advertising, we can devote more copy than ever to the positive aspects of our craft.

These times do not demand doing away with marketing. They demand marketing that pays its way. Only direct response can demonstrate that it does. If anyone should have the moxie to convince clients of that, direct marketers should.

Chapter 57

Attack of the TWABS II

Don't look now, but budget-cutters (aka Those Who Allocate Budgets, or TWABs) are greedily eyeing your department. And, in lean times, there is nothing quite like a marketing budget to set off their inner Pavlovian bell.

Good luck reasoning with them. You can try explaining that marketing creates sales. You protest that cutting back in a slow economy is like reducing insulin when a patient's diabetes worsens. It's a fair analogy, but in the midst of a recession an analogy is no match for a red pen.

It's tempting to dismiss undeterred budget-cutters as myopic. But maybe there's a deeper reason behind their seeming ruthlessness. Maybe they don't believe that marketing pays.

Their skepticism may not be completely unwarranted. A good deal of today's marketing reporting is based on indirect indicators like recall, awareness, points, share, surveys, web hits, tweets, awards, etc., yet marketing campaigns scoring high in these areas routinely fail. To take just one example, can you name the fast food chain that featured a spokes-Chihuahua? Extra credit if you recite the tagline in Spanish. Hint: Taco Bell, and *yo quiero Taco Bell*. Sales plummeted over the course of the campaign, which is why Taco Bell retired it in 2000. Yet even today people have no trouble recalling it.

So let's be fair. If you controlled the purse strings, I hope that you wouldn't settle for indirect evidence any more than a TWAB should.

Since sales can rise and fall for reasons other than marketing, sales alone are also an indirect indicator. Consider firearms marketers in the U.S. whose sales surged beginning in late 2008. Somehow I suspect credit goes less to marketing efforts and more to silly rumors that on the heels of his inauguration President Obama was going to nix the Second Amendment.

Fending off budget-cutters requires a better argument than "Everyone knows marketing sells" or even "Sales are up." You're going to need incontrovertible evidence that your marketing produces a positive Return On Investment. And you're going to have to prove that the positive ROI would not have occurred on its own.

Thank goodness for properly executed direct response marketing, which comes with its own bulletproof, empirical evidence. A properly managed direct response program can stand you on solid ground before the fiercest TWAB. Here are some tips for building such a program, and for ensuring that the ground under you remains firm:

1. Keep up with what works. Know what other direct marketers are testing and learning. Develop a peer network for sharing information. Read direct response books and periodicals. Then, when a budget-cutter asks why you spend the company's dollars the way you do, you'll have an empirical leg to stand on.

2. *Test before you bet the farm.* Test markets, offers, and creative executions. When you find out what sells the most at the lowest cost, roll it out.

3. *Test after betting the farm, too.* Once you have a winning campaign, keep testing new variations. You may stumble upon a nuanced or new approach that works even better.

4. *Track results responsibly.* Do not stand for generalities like, "Response was over the top." Know how much you sold, how much you spent selling it, and how much revenue it produced. Bean counters, who rarely encounter such precision from marketers, will be impressed.

5. *Know and factor in the lifetime value of respondents.* Most new customers are worth more than one sale. Calculate ROI on the revenue that a new customer represents over time.

6. *Use control groups.* Sooner or later, someone will suggest that sales would have gone up on their own, without spending on marketing. Control groups—people not exposed the marketing—provide a rock-solid defense. When a control group buys at a lesser rate than a test group, it's clear that your campaign made the difference.

7. *Admit flops.* When you do, management is more likely to believe your reports of success.

8. *Adapt fast.* Don't waste money giving failures chance after chance. Change something and try again.

9. Keep management sold. Find non-whiny ways to inform management about the scientific nature of direct response, and of your results. Invite a bean-counter or two to lunch on occasion and do the same. Who knows? Next time there's a crunch, maybe they'll leave your budget alone and instead go after sensitivity training, positive thinking seminars, retreats, and ropes courses. As they should, budget crunch or not.

10. Know when to call a pro. Heroes know when to call for reinforcements. If you need outside help, seek it.

Chapter 58

Right and Wrong Ways to Brag About Your Success

I hope you need no reminder that direct response marketing is the original measurable form of advertising. Direct response doesn't require inferring success from gains in awareness, recall, and name recognition, nor does it offer that luxury. People either respond or they don't. Should results disappoint, there is no place to hide. All the more reason to celebrate, even brag about, our stunning wins.

And brag we should. Press releases, blogs, and other forms of self-promotion aren't just for the PR department. They offer great ways to share what we learn, attract new clients, and grow the industry. In moments of unguarded candor, we might also admit to enjoying just a smidge of ego gratification.

A word of caution: how we express our successes can undermine or enhance the brand perception of direct response.

A time-honored practice is to express direct response results in terms of percent-of-target-who-respond. It's not unusual for practitioners to say, "Our program pulled a response of x percent." This usually elicits a gasp of wonder, oft followed by an uninformed comment along the line of, "That's great. I mean, I always heard that y percent is considered really good."

Though it can be tempting to agree so as not to ruin a rare moment of basking in unabated admiration, there may be some benefit in resisting the temptation and setting the record straight instead.

A response is "good" only if it returns a profit. If you need a 3.25 percent response to break even, then three percent isn't so good. On the other hand, if you can break even with response of just 0.01 percent, you would be within your rights to throw a wild party in celebration of a 0.02 percent response.

Setting that particular record straight is no mere obsessive-compulsive nod to pedantry. Giving standard-status to an arbitrary number risks priming employers and clients to be disappointed, profitability aside, with anything less. The last thing a direct response marketing pro needs is for a profitable program to be deemed "weak" because it fell short of a folkloric milestone.

I suggest expressing results not in terms of a percent but in terms of Return On Investment (ROI). Suppose that a mailing of 200,000 pieces costing $90,000 brings in 5,000 responses accounting for $100,000 in revenue. Consider how much more relevant, informative and compelling it is to say "the campaign earned an 11 percent gross profit" than to say "it pulled a one-quarter percent response."

Trumpeting success is a good thing. But trumpeting it in terms of ROI helps demonstrate the real power of direct response marketing. Which, I submit, is an even better thing.

Chapter 59

What's a Good Response?

If you have ever touted direct response marketing's ability to deliver empirical results, you know about The Inevitable Question. Almost on cue, as you rhapsodize about testing, tracking, analysis, and predictive results, the client will train a hairy eyeball on you and ask, "What's a good response? One percent? Two? Three?" Caution: Framed in that manner, The Inevitable Question becomes an unintended trick question.

The direct response marketing industry holds up no percentage as its universal standard. Rather, a "good" response is one that achieves your objective. If your objective happens to be a response of one percent, then a "good" response starts at one percent. If you require 17 percent, "good" starts there. If for every thousand pieces mailed you need only one response, then 0.1 percent is "good."

With that in mind, it might be a good idea to set an objective or two before creating and launching your campaign. Obvious? I agree. But I have seen companies launch costly campaigns without regard for such details, only to flounder about trying to measure success afterward. That's like a throwing a dart nowhere in particular and then trying to evaluate your aim. Some companies wait until results come in and then set their objectives to match. That's like throwing a dart nowhere in particular, painting a target where it happens to stick, and bragging that you hit a bulls-eye.

If you are afflicted with the integrity to resist such folly, here's a saner approach to determining a good response:

1. Project the cost of your campaign. Since I'm no math wiz, let's keep it simple by assuming that you plan to spend $1,000.

2. Calculate the profit you will clear, on average, with every response. Again for the sake of my poor, tired brain, let's say that each response will bring you $100 in revenue.

3. Aha! You need only 10 responses to break even (10 responses x $100 = $1,000). That means that if you reach 1,000 people, just one percent will be a good response. If you reach 2,000 people, one-half of one percent will be good. If you reach 2,000 people and each respondent makes two purchases, then a response of a mere quarter of one percent will be good. And so on.

Upon completing the math, the owner of the hairy eyeball may say, "Now that I know the response I need, before going much further I'd like to know what response I'm going to get."

You cannot promise a specific result without testing, but there is a way to determine if the required response falls within the realm of possibility. Find out if your product or service has been sold using direct response before. If so, a track record may exist for grounding expectations in reality. Books, articles and the Internet may yield such information. While you're at it, start networking and trading information with others in the field. I have had great luck simply by asking seasoned pros to share their experience.

Even with historical data on your side, it's wise to test before committing big dollars. That's because no two products, creative approaches, or sets of market conditions are alike. Try your campaign on a small but representative, statistically valid market sample. If the sample responds at the desired level, repeat the test with another valid sample. If results hold, you can be reasonably sure they will also hold when you take the campaign market-wide.

Once you've determined what constitutes a good response, be sure to clue in the boss ahead of time. Otherwise, The Inevitable Question may rear its ugly head after the fact. The last thing you need is a boss who expresses dismay because a great result sounds unimpressive when expressed as a percentage.

Chapter 60

Why Clients Get The Work They Deserve

(And how to deserve the work you want)

I f you're a client and have never heard the axiom, "Clients get the advertising they deserve," either you don't get out much or your agency's people mind their tongues when you're around. But then, given that we creative types adapt to tongue-minding as naturally as house cats adapt to pearl-diving, only someone who doesn't get out much would even entertain the latter possibility.

The axiom has endured ever since that prolific wit Anonymous first uttered it. But does it hold water? I was a client the first time I heard it, and I have to tell you I didn't much care for the sound of it. It seemed as if agencies were trying to blame their failures on ... well, me. Now, after 30 years of working on both the client and agency sides, I believe Anonymous was onto something.

There is no need to assume that, by "the advertising you deserve," Anonymous meant only bad advertising. If your agency delivers work that you like and that nails objectives, good for you. You deserve it.

But you also deserve it if your agency persistently misses the mark. Even if you have an incompetent agency—they happen—you're not off the hook. When advertisers complain of "always having to redo the agency's work," I usually answer, not tactfully, "That either means you have a lousy agency, you're a lousy client, or both." One prospect actually paused and said, "You know, I think maybe we *are* a lousy client."

"Lousy client" isn't nearly as direct as I could be. I could as well say, "Either you won't fire a bad agency, you can't resist tinkering with good work, you give poor direction, you're just plain mean, or a combination of the above. In any of these cases, you're a lousy client and you get the lousy advertising you deserve."

Let's take these in reverse order.

—*If you're just plain mean,* that is, you like to bully, no agency will please you. Sadly, you may have little motivation to change, since your agency and your employees earn their living acting as if they like you.

—*If you can't resist tinkering,* you will most likely first need to deal with denial. There is a wide gulf between pointing out bona fide errors for the agency to correct and obsessive tinkering, but said gulf masquerades as a fine line. I once sat for 30 minutes while a client mulled changing "happy," which was buried in body copy, to "pleased." Another client stopped a printing press to remove a period after a headline, because he'd gotten it in his head that headlines shouldn't end in periods. Another, who wanted justified type but couldn't abide hyphens, tied up an art director with endless, needless kerning. Another needlessly delayed a direct mail launch twice: Once to personally review and approve the pattern to be printed inside a safety envelope; and again to personally view and approve a standard rate postage stamp.

Obsessive-compulsive tinkering has little or no effect on sales, but works wonders for sapping morale and driving up costs. Here are two recommendations before questioning whether the agency is up to snuff:

1. *Know what matters.* You will not increase sales by changing "like" to "such as," enlarging the logo, or not using a preposition to end a sentence with.

2. *Set aside your personal preferences.* When you evaluate creative work, do not ask yourself, "How would I have done this?" Ask, "Regardless of how I would have done this, does the approach work?" If the answer is that it works, get out of the way and approve it.

Learn to let go, or your advertising will never rise above what you would have done on your own, which rather negates the point of hiring an agency, and results in naught but the advertising you deserve.

—*If you give your agency poor direction,* the cure is a rock-solid strategy. With your agency's participation, define your target market, objectives, incentive offer, key claim, copy points, and overall tone. This provides a stationary target for your agency. Hold to it when it's time to evaluate work. You can also help by being up-front about any peculiarities of your organization's inner workings and the personal agendas of decision influencers.

—*If you won't fire a bad agency,* I sort of understand. Besides the fact that finding and bringing on a new agency is a pain, dismissing your agency can put people you care about out of a job. So first, please be sure the problem isn't you. Review the above-referenced points with all the self-honesty you can muster. Otherwise, you will be doomed to trade hampering one agency for hampering another.

If the evidence points to the agency, level with the shop's principals. Explain your frustrations. Lay out expectations. For their part, the agency may need to air a concern or two about you. Together, decide if it's worth another try. Beyond that, if the need for a change becomes abundantly clear, face up to it. If you do nothing to improve the agency's performance yet you won't replace it, you get the advertising you deserve.

If you're getting great work out of your agency, pat yourself on the back. You are getting the work you deserve. You might consider patting the agency on the back, too. But if you'd like the work to improve, it's going to be up to you to deserve it.

Chapter 61

Programs Schmrograms

I just spotted another—yes, ANOTHER—customer service program called "We Care."

This one has all the trimmings. It had cute plastic "I care" pins with cheap gold paint flaking off the corners. It had a wall poster showing an inverted pyramid with the wide part at the top marked "customers" and the narrow triangle at the bottom marked "CEO" and employees and managers falling somewhere in-between and a line underneath saying something about customers reigning supreme.

None of the above seemed to have much effect on the clerk who was seated behind the counter, wearing the pin upside down, and carrying on an extended personal phone call while avoiding looking up at the customer.

When Wee (not a typo) Care runs its course, management will likely buy or invent another program called "We're Here For You When It's Convenient," "E-x-c-e-l-l-e-n-c-e Spells Excellence," "Empowering For Empowerment," or perhaps an acronym like "Total Organization Intuitive Lasting Excellence Training Systems."

These programs have their good points, but not for the companies that buy and implement them. They provide revenues for the companies that produce them. Implementing them rarely does more than delude insulated CEOs into believing they're doing something positive about customer service.

Only those rare CEOs who have not allowed themselves to become strangers to the battlefield tend not to buy these programs. Nor do they appear to need them.

I know a bank CEO who works in the teller line when things get busy. He gives his direct phone number out freely, and instructs his secretary not to screen callers.

I know a department store manager who, when a department is overwhelmed, works side-by-side with the help on the sales floor until things are back under control.

I know a manager who calls her people out of the blue to say things like, "Just wanted you to know I think you did a great job with that customer this morning."

Oddly enough, customer-orientation in these organizations manages to filter down by itself, without assistance from programs.

If you have a customer service problem, don't waste time and resources attacking it at the point of sale. What happens there reflects what your people perceive matters to you. They arrive at their perceptions from what you practice, not from what you preach, not from programs, and not from reading your message in the company newsletter that someone in PR wrote for you.

To motivate employees, don't give them a program. Give them a role model.

Chapter 62

Don't Hire Expertise If You're Going to Overrule It

Last week I recommended to a prospective client that we not work together. I am not given to saying no to revenue, so you may wonder what I was thinking. In case the prospective client wondered, too, I explained it as tactfully as I could:

> The reason I'd rather not work together at this time is that, and I think you'll agree, you have a kitchen with enough chefs with enough say to keep me from using the best of my expertise. Both of us would most likely waste time and lose money, and the finished work would inevitably be compromised. Let's not do that to you or me.

I didn't enjoy doing that. I liked the fellow, his product, the way he went about selling it, and the way he treated his customers. But I have learned the hard way not to accept clients who think they know better than I or, in this case, who defer to a committee who think they know better than I.

To be sure, they may indeed know better than I. No matter. Whether they do or think they do, the result will be a compromised project with both sides taking credit for a good outcome or placing blame for a bad one.

Do not visit a restaurant only to tell the chef to step aside while you make your own dinner.

Chapter 63

Why Attorneys Shouldn't Write Sales Letters

A law firm retained me to write a sales letter. After I did, they complained that it was deceptive. "When you make a form letter appear to be too personalized," the memo said, "it comes across as misleading and more personalized than it actually is."

This was my not too tactful reply:

> A personal tone is deceptive? Come on. A major problem with your existing materials is precisely that they read like form letters. No wonder response is low! There is no deception in making any communication feel personal, even when you send it to millions. Presumably, that is why you engaged the likes of the RESPONSE Agency instead of having an attorney or paralegal do the writing.
>
> To cast a bit of light on the method backing my madness, here is some perspective from this alleged direct response mail expert. The assignment was to craft a sales letter to outperform the existing one. In order of clout, here are the top three tested and proven strategic pegs for effective direct mail:
>
> Peg 1: Reach the right prospects. You have this one covered, having already engaged with and qualified recipients by phone. Since the list cannot be improved upon, all we have left to work with are Pegs 2 and 3.

Peg 2: Extend a compelling incentive offer. The incentive offer ranks second because it makes the difference between "I should do this someday" and "Yikes! If I act now I get the free widget!" You'd be amazed at the power a gift wields, but since it appears that a bona fide gift is not to be, all we have left to work with is Peg 3.

Peg 3: Use proven creative techniques. "Proven" is no overstatement, provided you find yourself a genuine direct mail pro and not one of the charlatans in abundant supply. Direct mail—responsible direct mail, anyway—was built by testing against controls. A warm, first-person letter, one page or longer, conversational language, and short paragraphs matter. So does a compelling P.S., for it is usually read first. So do things like double-spacing between paragraphs, double-indented paragraphs, and indented first lines on paragraphs. And so does creating the impression of one-to-one communication from a real person who gives a damn about the reader. Which, you have assured me, you do.

Let's not weaken the only peg you have left by making the language less personal.

Not surprisingly, my first project for them was also my last. To their credit, they paid their bill without a fuss.

Chapter 64

Résumé Advice

Sometimes people request résumé advice as a ploy for getting an executive to review and consider it. Taking Heather's request for feedback at face value, I wrote the following bona fide critique. She didn't write back.

Dear Heather:

As promised, I have looked over your résumé from the perspective of an employer who happens to be a marketing guy. I hope you'll find something useful here that makes your résumé stand out, so that prospective employers will hound you and offer to shower you with exorbitant salaries.

You've done a good job of following the format most schools suggest for résumés. Therein lies the problem. Employers like me are buried in résumés that look like what schools suggest, meaning every résumé we get is a clone of the last one we looked at. And that means every résumé we look at bores us just like the last one.

So, my first suggestion is that you put some thought into how to make your résumé, or, rather, how to make *you* stand out in the most positive light possible. I'm not so much talking about cute borders or innovative uses of type, though layout can certainly be a factor. I'm talking about using your words and format to make your unique abilities and personality jump off the page at your reader. The less effort it takes an employer to figure out what makes you great and unusual, the better off you are.

A résumé is usually approached as a form: a document that has to have certain things in certain places. I would suggest dumping the form approach for the marketing approach. Your résumé is a sales pitch. It is your one shot at getting an employer to take a serious look at you. To be sure, this is no time to go hog wild, but it's also no time to subject a prospective employer to yet another cloned résumé.

Setting aside theory, here are some specific recommendations:

—Every résumé opens with "Objective." And every objective on every resumé says exactly the same thing ("... to utilize my skills ... challenging position ... personal growth ..."), which means they all say nothing. I'd do away with the Objective if I were you. Your objective is to get a job, and your prospective employer already knows that.

—Don't believe anyone who tells you to keep your résumé to a single page. Take the space you need to sell yourself—no less, and, above all, no more. Just make sure that every word is necessary. People will read a long résumé that's fascinating and relevant, but they'll trash one that's merely long. When I last updated my résumé some 30 years ago, it ran five pages. I bet yours could run to two with no problem.

—If you use white space, such as double returns between paragraphs, you will increase readership.

—Your Awards/Achievements section is impressive. I can't help thinking how much more impressive it might be if you translated each point into a benefit for the prospective employer. For instance, what good does it do my company that you were a Collegiate Softball Athlete for the University of Utah on a four-year scholarship? I'm sure it indicates something about your character and sense of commitment or willingness to work hard and succeed against all odds, but you would do well to succinctly spell it out for employers lacking the imagination or inclination to infer it. If you go to a two-page résumé, you'll have room.

—Likewise, when you participated in various community events, what skills or character traits did you develop that I'll find useful?

—Likewise, point out how your sports background can benefit an employer: your commitment to hard work despite pain, your focus on attaining the goal, your healthy competitive spirit, etc.

—Your résumé makes clear your passion for sports. Nothing wrong with that, since that's who you are, but you might want to round it out. Do you also like reading to handicapped kids, playing the theremin in your spare time, or sculpting?

—About that line, "Loves to work with people." Until more résumés say, "I prefer the company of housebroken squirrels," it's a throwaway line. Instead, you might show me *how* you work with people. For instance, are you skilled at conflict resolution, able to adapt to a wide variety of working conditions, able to coach without putting people on the defensive, or able to take advice without feeling personally attacked?

To sum up: *stand out*. That is, stand out in a positive way. Wearing a clown suit to a fine restaurant will make you stand out, but it won't get you a table. So perhaps I should say, *build your résumé so that, at a glance, what makes you unique, invaluable, and indispensable stands out.*

Chapter 65

Possibly Overpriced Free Advice for Career Hopefuls

For a school assignment, an impressive young man needed to obtain advice from an executive on landing a job. Here is what I wrote for him.

On having a degree

I differ from other employers on this one. I don't care if you have a degree. I know brilliant, non-college educated people, and I know PhDs who are dumber than a box of rocks. I have hired two creative directors, one with a master's degree, the other with no college at all. I have a BA. My son has no college and is an immensely successful businessperson. His secret? A rare combination of talent, tenacity, and, thank goodness, ethics. But no college.

An undergraduate degree is not so much a door-opener as the lack of one is a door-closer. You must bring more than a degree with you if you want an employer to take you on.

Things I look for

I look for how a candidate will fit in with me, my team, and my clients.

Dress, grooming, and manners matter. I don't want clients to lose confidence at first sight.

I look for someone who has done a bit of homework on me and my shop. Mine is a different approach. Those who trouble to learn about it start with the advantage.

An over-confident applicant is off-putting, and an under-confident one is either wimpy or acting coy, and neither impresses. Teachability is a good indicator.

So is determination. I recall a young college graduate who showed up cold, résumé in hand, hoping to be an account executive. He was bright, qualified, and likable, and he presented well. Unfortunately, our only opening was for a receptionist. He swallowed hard and said, "I'll take a job scrubbing floors if it gets me in." He was the best receptionist we ever had and went on to a great career.

The creative person I seek is hard to find and a far cry from what most agencies are looking for. Too many people go into advertising because at heart they are not marketers but artistes, and it's easier to break into advertising than into Hollywood. They will create award-winning work, which is a priority to most clients and agencies. Not to me.

If you see "Account Executive" on a RESPONSE Agency employee's business card, know that internally I call that position "salesperson." I don't care that it is counter-cultural. I want someone who can pound the pavement, bring in new clients, and grow the clients we have by taking great care of them. That person is a rare bird. I have been lucky enough to have hired three in the 22 years I've had my business.

Some ad agency people tell me that having "salespeople" is unprofessional. I find that not a little ironic.

The folly of "I can help you think up ideas"

Creative work is fun, so it's no wonder that a lot of people want to do it. It's not unusual for hopefuls to say, "I can help you think up ideas." They might as well say, "I have cool concepts for short films where I bet we could work in a product mention." It betrays naiveté about the advertising business. On-target ideas require up-front homework. Lots of it. The idea is the last step. You cannot walk in off the street and expect to "help think up ideas."

Moreover, I spend less than one percent of my time thinking up ideas. Advertising is a creative business, but the business aspect consumes far more of my time than the creative end does.

In the first interview

Do not ask me about holidays, hours, paid leave, vacation, health care, and other benefits. I offer those things, but I am looking for someone who cares more about helping me grow my business than when the next three-day weekend happens to be. If holidays et al matter to you, there are other ways to obtain the information. You may have heard of the Internet.

I like candidates who know what they want to do, and who understand from my point of view how they'll be an asset.

Even though deep down one or two of us may actually possess a latent trace of niceness, employers do not hire to be nice, but to build a business.

A caution about taking my advice

Please note where I have pointed out how I differ from other employers. I don't want you someday to blow a real interview in front of someone who doesn't think like me.

Chapter 66

Channeling Orwell

The management of a company whose business I would soon resign had just proudly shown me their new sales video. I cannot describe how bad it was. Not just poorly produced, it was offensive. The next thing I knew, they were pressing me for praise. I did my best to keep my reservations to myself, but I'm not good at that sort of thing. In no time, they had wormed out of me a quiet, reluctant, "I have some concerns." This raised their ire.

My concerns were promptly validated when customers, especially women, complained that the video was offensive. It was then that management informed me that the video had never been intended as a sales video. It was a training video.

When it became apparent that the video didn't train, management informed me that the video had not been intended as a training video any more than as a sales video. It was an internal morale-boosting video.

Meanwhile, their account of my quiet "I have some concerns" evolved into an epic tale of my having thrown a tantrum in their office.

This happened in 1986. Were I as Orwellian as they, I would improve the story by changing the year to 1984.

Chapter 67

Books and Articles on Success Secrets Are Dumb

When I was approached for an interview about my views on success, my first impulse was to decline. Who says I'm successful? By whose standard? Who am I to presume to lecture on the subject?

I saw that Question 1 would let me define success. How convenient. There is no surer way to success than to create its definition in your own image.

You may suspect by now that I have little regard for the "success industry." In this case, "I have little regard" is to be understood to mean "I think it's for the most part silly, a waste of time, and useless, hollow cheerleading."

Take Question 4: "When faced with adversity, what pushes you to keep moving forward?" A look through previous answers yielded rah-rah gems like "quitting isn't an option," would-be humble profundities like "the illumination from the lanterns held by others," and the oxymoronic "by not letting 'no' be part of my vocabulary."

I went ahead with the interview with the hope of providing something besides the usual fluff. I leave you to judge whether I pulled off the substance thing or merely played the snarky contrarian.

Q: How do you define success?

A: The fact that you would lead with this question shows just how conveniently abstract that word "success" is. If we were talking about lima beans, you wouldn't need to lead with, "How do you define lima bean?" Egotists and wimps define success to ensure that they qualify; defeatists define it to ensure that they don't. I like to define success as living in sync with one's character and values.

Q: What is the key to success?

A: Success is found in living your values. You cannot control outcomes; all you can be assured of is that you did your best with what you had at any given time. Provided, of course, that you truly did.

Q: Did you always know you would be successful?

A: This begs the question as to whether I'm successful. It also begs the question as to whether it's possible to know in advance that you will succeed. You may have a positive attitude, but that is no predictor of a successful life. This would be more apparent if the likes of Jack Canfield and Rhonda Byrne gave equal time in their silly books to positive thinkers who died hopeless, poverty-stricken wretches. Actions and attitude matter, but acknowledging serendipity provides a much-needed foundation for compassion and humility.

Q: What makes a great leader?

A: Understanding the difference between bullying and leading, and tending toward the latter.

*Q: **When faced with adversity, what pushes you to keep moving forward?***

A: Sometimes it's sheer will. Sometimes it's sheer stupidity. Sometimes it's both, otherwise known as stubbornness. On a good day, I combine will with wisdom, otherwise known as "vision." Speaking of wisdom, moving forward isn't always wise. Sometimes it's wise to move sideways or backwards, try another route, or recognize an ill-fated or ill-conceived journey and abandon it.

*Q: **What is the greatest lesson you've ever learned?***

A: Two come to mind: (1) My happiness is my job and no one else's. (2) When evidence contradicts intuition, trust evidence.

*Q: **What do you enjoy doing in your spare time?***

A: Learning, reading, writing, thinking, playing the piano, composing, napping, walking my dog, and forcing people to look at pictures of my grandchildren.

*Q: **What advice would you give to college students about entering the workforce?***

A: Before deciding that you are smarter than the old pros, take care to ensure that you are not mistaking naiveté for vision. Listen, learn, get the lay of the land. You will have plenty of time to take the world by storm.

Part Twelve

Fundamentals

Chapter 68

12 Tips for Stronger Writing

1. Write to communicate, not to impress with your writing. Good writers disappear behind what they bring to life.

2. Say it shorter.

Weak: *She was so confused, she didn't know what to do.*
Stronger: *She was stumped.*

3. Small words beat big ones. Big words often signal a writer trying to show off (see Rule 1).

Weak: *Masticate.* Stronger: *Chew.*

Weak: *Expectorate.* Stronger: *Spit.*

Weak: *Inebriate.* Stronger: *Drunk.*

4. Active is stronger than passive voice.

Weak: *He was being watched by everyone.*
Stronger: *Everyone watched him.*

5. Beware "is," "are," "was" and "were." They may signal an opportunity for condensing.

Weak: *She was well-liked.*
Stronger: *People liked her.*
Weak: *The recipe is a combination of ...*
Stronger: *The recipe contains ...*

6. Forget what your English teacher said about not using "you," "your," etc. In real writing, use "you" freely, but intelligently. With some admitted exceptions, addressing the reader as "the reader" or the customer as "the customer" is punishable by death.

Weak: *The reader will appreciate ...*

Stronger: *You'll love ...*

7. Edit like mad. Throw out every word you can without losing meaning.

Weak: *He told everyone present that his motive for killing the late canary was the inescapable result of a considerable number of mishaps during his childhood.*

Stronger: *He blamed killing the canary on his childhood.*

8. Beware adverbs. Chances are you can do better with a stronger verb.

Weak: *He walked slowly.*

Stronger: *He lumbered.*

Or: *He crept.*

Or: *He shuffled.*

Or: *He lurched.*

Or: *He moped.*

9. Don't tell. Show.

Telling: *He was mad.*

Showing: *His face reddened, his fists tightened, his jaw trembled. Smoke billowed from his ears.*

10. Avoid "got," "get," etc. They signal a need for better sentence structure or a better verb.

> Weak: *He got hungry, so he got in the car, got to the diner, and got lunch.*
>
> Stronger: *His stomach growling, he drove to the diner and ordered lunch.*

11. Avoid clichés.

> Weak: *He settled into bed, snug as a bug in a rug, and lived happily ever after.*
>
> Stronger: *He slipped under the covers and turned off the light.*

12. Loosen up. Use conversational English. Don't be afraid of contractions. Or fragments. Even the stuffiest PhD prefers an accessible voice to one that is mindlessly formal. Just don't overdo it.

Chapter 69

PowerPoint Presentations Need Not Be Painfully Dull: 10 Tips

Any fool can create a boring PowerPoint presentation, which is why so many fools do. You need only paste lengthy excerpts from your speech onto your slides in type too small to read, cram as many photos, charts, graphs and diagrams as possible onto a single slide, use lots of animation just because you can, glue your eyes to your notes, speak in a monotone, remember to say "ummm" or "uhhhh" as often as you can, and, whatever else you do, never, ever rehearse.

But for renegades who wish to engage the audience, here are some tips for doing a PowerPoint right.

1. Don't begin by writing what you intend to say. I'll tell you when it's time to start writing. For now, focus on concepts you wish to convey.

2. Look for ways to convey concepts visually. Many presenters seem to forget that slides are visual. A slide that repeats what you're saying may be appropriate now and then, but slides that illustrate rather than parrot drive points home. Suppose you want to talk about anger. Instead of a slide that says "Anger," try showing a photo of a cat bearing fangs, a red-faced person, a steaming teapot, or an erupting volcano.

3. Surprise 'em every 9 minutes. No matter how good you are, people tend to tune out about every 10 minutes—unless you give them a reason not to. So every 9 minutes or less, introduce a visual with what I like to call "head-scratcher" value: an unexpected image that will make sense only when you explain it. Partway through one of my marketing presentations, I show a cartoon-illustration of a microscopic germ. What does the germ have to do with marketing? That's the point. You have to listen to find out.

4. Use slides and remarks to create synergy. To illustrate the ineffectiveness of trying to illuminate minds by means of brow-beating, in a recent presentation I *showed* a photo of a baseball bat and I *said*, "This is not a light switch." It was well-received. (How do I know? See Point 10 below.) Neither the slide nor the statement alone conveyed much, but together they communicated with power. So effectively, I might add, that there was no need to say more on that particular point. I moved on, and my audience stayed with me.

5. Never use word slides as a default visual. Sure, sometimes for emphasis it's appropriate to display a key phrase, word for word, as you speak it. But most of the time, avoid word slides. They usually signal that you need to work harder to communicate visually.

6. Remember that no one can read a screen filled with type. Nor will anyone try.

7. Overkill kills. Once you've made a point, move on. The only time to return to it is in a recap or to reinforce an ongoing theme. If you're an obsessive-compulsive personality type like me, you'll find that this one takes discipline.

8. If you have figured out how to convey your concepts visually, now it's time to start writing what you will say. Something magical may happen, namely, your visuals and remarks will set up and play off of each other. You're on your way to an engaging presentation.

9. Rehearse. Smooth speakers aren't smooth by accident. They rehearse, rehearse, and rehearse. Besides smoothing your delivery, rehearsing will also help you avoid committing the deadly speaking sin of *going over your allotted time*. I am often surprised at the number of one-hour talks that take two, and how often "just five minutes more" takes 30. Audiences hate speakers who take liberties with their time.

10. Look up at your audience now and then. If you rehearse, you'll be better able to tear your eyes from your notes. Constant eye contact with your audience isn't mandatory, but the occasional look around is. There are two reasons for this. One, audiences like being spoken with more than they like being read to. Two, you can benefit from immediate feedback. If you see yawns, eyes wandering, slouching, or people whispering and passing notes instead of focusing on what you're yammering on about, you can change your pace or tone and vow to prepare something better next time. Keeping your eyes glued to your notes robs you of any chance to improve.

Chapter 70

Why It's "Test, Test, Test" and Not Just "Test"

Most direct response professionals will tell you that the key to success is to *test, test, test*. They really do say it three times, just like that. It's that important.

Rather than bet the whole budget on an unproven strategy, first test it on a representative sample. Then watch what the sample does—or doesn't do—as a result. In no time, you'll know whether to embrace or abandon the proposed strategy.

Even better, try split testing. Expose one sample of your market to one version of your ad and another sample to another. This is a useful way to settle just about any question: which headline to use, which color is best, what photos work best, which market is most responsive, and more.

Testing requires discipline. It means cooling your jets until the facts are in. It can also mean discovering that the approach you like best isn't the most effective. Wise marketers set aside personal preferences and let market behavior speak for itself.

Chapter 71

"No One Gives a [Bleep] What You Want to Say"

F inding and reaching your target market aren't the same thing. *Finding* your target market has to do with locating customers and prospective customers and then identifying the media they're likely to consume. *Reaching* your target market has to do with connecting in a way that makes them more likely to receive your message and, hopefully, act on it.

The first step to reaching customers is to observe the customers you already have. What kinds of products do they buy most often? Do most of your customers fall within a certain age range? How about their income range? Do they shop from work or home? Where do they live or work? How do they dress? What class of car do they drive? Do they pay with cash, checks, plastic cards, NFC, Apple Pay, Google Wallet, or other technology? Is English their first or second language? What are their political leanings? What do they seem to value— Thrift? Status? Convenience? Luxury?

These observations will provide insights into how they think and feel, so you can reach them with messages that are relevant and motivating. The trick is to set aside what matters to *you* in favor of what matters to *them*. You may be enamored of your biodegradable packaging, but if your customer cares more about an easy-grip handle, talk about that instead. You may want to talk about your remodeled showroom, but if your customer cares more about this month's two-for-one offer, talk about that instead. As the creative director of a competing ad agency once told a client, "That's just it. Not one gives a [bleep] what you want to say."

I might have fired him for speaking to a client that way, but he had a point.

Chapter 72

The Best Mailing List on the Market Isn't on the Market

A number of fine mailing lists are available for rent or purchase, but experts agree that the most valuable list to which you will ever mail is your house list, that is, a list of your own customers and prospects. Since the people on your house list already know and trust you, the experience of most direct marketers suggests that they are more likely than non-customers to purchase from you.

Building a house list is the first step toward true database marketing. Here's how to get your house list started.

Ask. Building a mailing list can be as easy as saying, "May I add you to our mailing list?" Don't be shy. You'd be surprised at the number of customers who want to hear from you.

Have a sign-up sheet. Set it out, in plain sight, near the register. Be sure to provide a pen, preferably one that works.

Set out a fishbowl for business cards. Many companies invite customers to toss their business card into a fishbowl for a chance at winning a prize. Unwise companies throw away the cards after the drawing. Wise ones add the information from the cards to a mailing list.

Check checks. Most checks display your customer's name and address. Before sending checks to the bank, be sure to add the information to your mailing list. Better hurry. Checks are an endangered species.

Include prospects. Everyone who shows an interest—not just people who purchase—deserves an invitation to join your mailing list. This includes people who stop by, phone, write or email with questions.

Ask for referrals. People who buy from you probably have friends with like tastes. Give them sign-up cards to share with their friends and they might just do it.

Keep notes. Away from public view (to protect privacy), jot down information that will help you send relevant communications to your customers. Note areas of interest, preferred brands, favorite colors, sizes, past purchases, purchase dates, frequency of visits, and whether the person is a customer or prospect. Thus when you have a new shipment of Item A or a special on Service B, you can easily identify the people on your list who most likely will appreciate knowing about it.

Mail to your list often. People like receiving advertising mail. They agreed to be on your list because they wanted to hear from you. Don't let them down. Mailing too infrequently only risks being forgotten.

Track responses. Note customers who reference or bring in your mailings. These people are responsive. You may want to increase the frequency of your mailings to them.

Chapter 73

Finding and Using Email and Mail Lists

Besides your house list described in the previous chapter, you may want to consider a commercially traded list. While there are catalogs from which you can order a list, a competent broker can save you time, help you avoid pitfalls, and recommend lists you might not find on your own.

There's no sure-fire way to find the list broker that's right for you. Moreover, some specialize in one sort of list, some in another. A good starting place? Ask for a referral from a direct marketer you respect.

The best way to help a list broker help you is to share as much information as possible about your product, the problem it solves, and the kind of person you believe is most likely to benefit from having your product. Your broker may have experience with related products and be able to recommend lists that might not otherwise have crossed your mind. A broker may also be able to tell you what kinds of companies have had success using specific lists.

Some lists are available for purchase, but the best ones are available only for rent. A rent-only list is a good sign, for it usually means someone is keeping it updated. Renting a list means that you don't own it, which means that if you plan to mail to it more than once, you should ask your broker for a "multiple-use" rate. Unauthorized re-use of a list is illegal. Don't think a list manager won't know. Most add names and addresses of people who will report what they receive and from whom. If they receive an unauthorized mailing, it can trigger legal consequences.

If your broker requires a sample of your mail or email before agreeing to rent you a list, that's a good sign, too. It means you're dealing with a company that screens would-be users of its lists for integrity.

Here are some questions to ask a list broker to increase your odds of obtaining a reliable list:

What is the source of the list? It may be a list of people who responded to offers from other companies, who subscribed to publications, who marked areas of interest on a warranty card, or whose names were compiled from public sources such as directories.

If it's an email list, was permission obtained? Emailing to people who haven't opted in can consign you to a junk or spam file, get you blacklisted by a server, and even land you in legal trouble.

Some marketers obtain permission to share email information with companies that the customer might presumably want to hear from. Pay attention to *how* such permission is obtained. A pre-clicked box that subscribers must unclick may not indicate willful opt-ins as much as inattention. Boxes that subscribers intentionally click are better, but don't hold your breath in hopes of performance. Whether or not you run afoul of the CAN-SPAM Act, your message may still be diverted to a junk or spam file, and a server may still blacklist you.

For those reasons, email is better suited to existing customers who have given you their information with the understanding that you send them promotional emails. For prospecting, use direct mail instead. Direct mail has no junk filters, no server will blacklist you for failing to obtain permission, and you won't have to worry about running afoul of the CAN-SPAM Act.

How is the list verified? If you learn that the manager of a list you're considering regularly mails, emails, and telephones the list and makes changes based on deliverability, open rates, and other forms of feedback, that's a good sign.

How often is the list updated? Addresses and other data change faster than you might think. The more often a list is updated, the better. Every six months should be the bare minimum. Every quarter is better.

Chapter 74

Keeping Email and Mail Lists Healthy

O nce a list is created, it would be nice if it stayed up-to-date all by itself. But people change their email addresses often. They also move. (They die, too, but I'm trying to keep things upbeat.) Street names, zip codes, and phone numbers change. Jobs and job titles change. All of the above happen more often than you'd think.

It's important to keep abreast of changes. It's a matter of common sense that no matter how compelling your offers and creative work may be, they will perform at their best only if they arrive before the right eyes. Here are some tips for keeping your list at its peak performance level:

For direct mail, use the NCOA file. People who move may forget to tell you, but they almost always remember to tell the U.S. Postal Service. The USPS maintains that information in its National Change of Address (NCOA) file. For a nominal fee, you can match this file against your own mailing list. It's one of the most efficient and painless ways to keep your mailing list up-to-date. If you prefer not to handle the update yourself, most letter shops will perform this service for you.

For direct mail, use RETURN SERVICE REQUESTED. Mail returned to you is an opportunity to update your records.

Placing the magic words "RETURN SERVICE REQUESTED" on the address-side of your direct mail informs the U.S. Postal Service that you wish to have misaddressed mail returned to you so that can make changes to your list accordingly. This gives you the chance to cut waste and update customer information.

Promptly remove names upon request. When people ask to be removed from your mailing list, do it. If it will take a few days to get the change through your system, tell them. Prompt compliance is good customer relations and, in the case of email lists, a legal requirement.

Invite customers to update their own information. Design online forms, catalog order forms, reply cards, and coupons so that customers can update their own information. The following language can work well: "We apologize for any errors in your information. Please correct below." A customer who takes the trouble to correct information and send it back to you is showing an interest in receiving more offers from you, so it's important to update the information immediately.

Part Thirteen

Marketing with a Conscience

Chapter 75

Disliking Advertising from an Informed Perspective

I wrote this article for Skeptical Inquirer, *a magazine dedicated to science and reason. You will be able to see that I was not addressing marketers but rather a more general audience. Still, I am surprised at the number of marketing and advertising profession-als who buy into the myths that I dispatch here.*

Quelle surprise. In yet another poll, 36 percent of re-spondents rated the "honesty and ethical standards" of advertising people "low/very low." It's a wonder Gal-lup bothers asking anymore. I'd take umbrage at the public's dim view of my profession were it not for one sticking point. Namely, that it isn't entirely unwarranted.

But it isn't entirely warranted, either, and it seems to me that if you're going to dislike what I do for a living, you may as well dis-like it from an informed perspective. Space and lethargy do not permit addressing every abuse laid to advertising's charge, so I shall deal with three that I hear most often: that advertising con-trols behavior; short of controlling, that advertising manipulates by unfair means; and that advertising lies at the root of many a societal ill. Then I shall wrap up with a look at an advertising abuse that I think could do with more outcry than it receives.

Claim: Advertising controls behavior

In 1957, marketing researcher James Vicary held report-ers rapt with results from an advertising experiment. Every five seconds for one-3000th of a second, Vicary had flashed "Hungry? Eat popcorn" and "Drink Coca-Cola" onscreen during showings of the movie *Picnic*. The flash was too brief for the conscious mind, but not for the subconscious. Over a six-week trial, Coke sales rose 18.1 percent. Popcorn sales rose 57.7 percent. So great was public outrage that hardly anyone noticed when, five years later, Vicary admitted to having made the whole thing up.

Conveniently published the same year Vicary held his press conference, Vance Packard's bestseller *The Hidden Persuaders* fanned the flame. Often deferring to Vicary's alleged expertise, the book served up terrifying gems like this:

> Housewives consistently report that one of the most pleasurable tasks of the home is making a cake ... James Vicary made a study of cake symbolism and came up with the conclusion that 'baking a cake traditionally is acting out the birth of a child' so that when a woman bakes a cake for her family she is symbolically presenting the family with a new baby, an idea she likes very much.

Or this:

> Mr. Vicary set up his cameras and started following the ladies as they entered the store. The results were startling, even to him ... The ladies fell into what Mr. Vicary calls a hypnoidal trance, a light kind of trance that, he explains, is the first stage of hypnosis ... the main cause of the trance is that the supermarket is packed with products that in former years would have been items that only kings and queens could afford, and here in this fairyland they were available.

Those damnable advertisers! Women who thought they were buying cake mixes were but sating an innate baby lust while lost in a hypnoidal trance.

Such nonsense hasn't gone away. The 2004 PBS documentary *The Persuaders* shows child-psychiatrist-turned-marketing-consultant Clotaire Rapaille advising a French company to sell cheese in America in resealable plastic pouches. The idea was not new. Rapaille could have advised his client, "Do what U.S. cheese marketers do, duh." Instead he produced a convoluted metaphor perhaps worthier of his hefty consulting fee:

> ... in America the cheese is dead, which means is pasteurized, which means legally dead and scientifically dead ... plastic is a body bag ... the fridge is the morgue; that's where you put the dead bodies ... in France the cheese is alive ... you never put the cheese in the refrigerator, because you don't put your cat in the refrigerator ...

Those damnable cheese marketers! Just as 1950s women could not resist birthing cakes, modern Americans cannot resist snacking on well-preserved corpses.

Journalism professor Wilson Bryan Key rekindled subliminal advertising fears in the 1970s. Key claimed that sexual images hidden in photos of everything from ice cubes to fried clams made consumers buy against their will. And no less than advertising industry icon David Ogilvy jumped on the mind-control bandwagon in 1983, when he wrote in his *Ogilvy on Advertising*:

I once myself came near to doing something so diabolical that I hesitate to confess it even now, 30 years later. Suspecting that hypnotism might be an element in successful advertising, I engaged a professional hypnotist to make a commercial. When I saw it in the projection room, it was so powerful that I had visions of millions of suggestible consumers getting up from their armchairs and rushing like zombies through the traffic on their way to buy the product at the nearest store. Had I invented the ultimate advertisement? I burned it, and never told my client how close I had come to landing him in a national scandal.

Evidence for hypnotism as a means of mind control is as lacking as evidence for Ogilvy's tale. He gave no account of testing the commercial's zombification power, only of being a horrified focus group of one. We cannot test the commercial for ourselves, because he allegedly put a match to the only copy. No writer, director, actor, lighting technician, editor, or even the hypnotist ever came forth. No raw footage or script ever surfaced. This anecdote smells of self-promotion à la Vicary.

If you wonder why an industry in the business of creating positive images would promote myths harmful to its own, consider that advertising agencies needn't appeal to consumers. Worse things could happen to an ad agency than for a client to believe it has magic powers. Yet if advertising really had such power, the best minds in the advertising business would not have produced market failures like the following, which I swear I'm not making up: Colgate frozen dinners, Bic disposable underwear, Cosmopolitan magazine yogurt, Mc-Donald's clothing, Ben-Gay aspirin, Smith & Wesson bicycles, Life Saver's soda, Frito-Lay lemonade, Harley-Davidson eau de toilette, New Coke, and even the popular Taco Bell Chihuahua.

Despite ample debunking and no evidence of effectiveness, subliminal advertising allegations persist. The reality is that if advertisers can control minds, they hide it well.

Laboratories, sex, and other delights

Some mind-control scares come out of laboratories. Subjects view ads, commercials, or web pages while hidden devices track their eye movements, an fMRI looks for brain areas that light up, or a machine measures their galvanic responses. Should eyes fixate or move, brain areas light up, pupils dilate, or skin temperatures change, the lab's PR department sends out a press release.

But there is a problem in leaping from "had an effect in a lab" to "made you buy in a marketplace." Early in my career I took over advertising for a company that marketed to the trucking industry. My predecessor had adorned ads with half-dressed women. I persuaded the company to let me substitute photos of trucks, combined with straight talk about the product. I suspect my predecessor's campaign would have produced more dilation, fixation, galvanic responses, and brain light-ups than mine. But in the real world, truckers quit hanging our ads on garage walls. Oh, and sales quadrupled.

The case is anecdotal, but its basis is not. I happened to know that the legendary John Caples, who built his career on controlled advertising tests, had written this in *Tested Advertising Methods*:

> Before the widespread use of readership surveys, some ad men believed that the way to stop a male reader was to show a picture of bathing beauty. Apparently this technique may create desire for the girl, but it does not seem to create desire for the product being advertised. ... One interesting observation that has come out of readership surveys is that men tend to look at ads containing pictures of men and that women tend to look at ads containing pictures of women ... A man figures that an ad containing a picture of a man is likely to be an ad for a man's product and that an ad containing a picture of a woman is likely to be for a woman's product.

The point is not to address whether sex sells, but to illustrate that a laboratory response is a far cry from an actual purchase.

A 2011 study gained some attention among skeptics. Priyali Rajagopal from Southern Methodist University and Nicole Votolato Montgomery from College of William and Mary found that advertising could convince people they had sampled popcorn that in fact they had not. If creating a false memory constitutes mind control, then there you have it. But note that the study did not demonstrate that the false memory made anyone buy anything. Given the poor track record of other laboratory findings in the real world, I have my doubts. It is easier to induce a response in a lab than to make someone rise from a chair and head to a store.

One reason laboratory tests tend not to prove predictive is that people do not experience advertising in a lab the way they do at home. In a lab, participants know they are being observed, which affects behavior. Moreover, they focus on the commercial or ad they are shown. At home, no one is observing them, and commercials and ads compete for attention with bathroom trips, phone calls, texting, tweeting, Minecraft, magazines, in-person conversation, muted sound, Facebook, scratching, channel surfing, web surfing, napping, you name it. Nor do families gather at the tube. The same household may have multiple TVs tuned to different stations or that stream commercial-free content.

With no evidence to support the alleged power of subliminal or hypnotic advertising, and no evidence suggesting that laboratory tests are predictive, you may think that charges of mind-controlling advertising look somewhat like garden-variety conspiracy theories. You may be on to something.

Claim: Advertising manipulates behavior

Use *manipulate* if you like, but I think a more apt term is *influence*. Advertising pleads guilty. This is not a little circular, since to influence is pretty much the point of advertising. But of course the real question is whether advertising goes about its task unfairly.

Let's start with the basic way advertising can influence. If you need new tires and see a tire dealer's flyer, you might visit that dealer. If you dropped your smart phone in the toilet, an ad for a waterproof phone might win your attention. If you're allergic to your eyeliner, an ad for a hypo-allergenic one might attract you. I hope you'll agree that influence of that sort is benign, possibly even useful. But then, those are products you might want. Advertising that influences you to buy products that you don't want is quite another matter. Isn't it a given that slicker, smoother, glitzier, better designed, more entertaining, and more memorable advertising can lodge itself in your mind so you'll reach for the advertised brand, want it or not, without knowing why? Why else would advertising agencies boast of work that is creative, original, memorable, and likable? Why else would clients keep spending big money on slick, creative ads?

Beware assuming that advertising people make rational decisions. Advertisers tend to deem a campaign successful if it "tested well" in a focus group, was recalled by a respectable percentage of a target market, won awards, or coincided with a sales increase. That focus groups are not predictive, remembered campaigns fail and not-remembered ones succeed, awards have no bearing, and correlation does not mean causation should make sense to most critical thinkers, but it does not to many an advertiser.

An exception is direct response advertising, a subset that concerns itself less with brand recognition and more with measured actions. More than a century of controlled direct response tests has revealed consistencies in marketplace behaviors. Want more people to click a link? Spell out, "click here to ..." Want to increase readership? Avoid light type on a dark background. Want more people to open your snail mail? Use an unusual envelope. Want more people to call a number on the TV? Avoid Prime Time. Want more people to take action? Offer a freebie for a limited time. Direct response advertising has thousands of such "rules."

Do not be misled. Most direct response rules, such as avoiding the use of light type on a dark background, do not so much win buyers as avoid losing them. And "more people" typically refers to incremental gains. It is not unusual for a direct response advertiser to celebrate when one percent of a target market takes a desired action. Boasts of "doubling sales" can mean going from "99 percent didn't buy" to "98 percent didn't buy." Response rates of two, three or more percent are not unheard-of, but every uptick waxes increasingly aspirational. This is a poor showing indeed for a would-be manipulator.

Equally telling is that direct marketers achieve their greatest gains by fine-tuning reaching the right audience and offering the right gift incentive. Fine-tuning creative work, the alleged stuff of manipulation, receives lowest priority. Many direct marketers hold that creative work accounts for only 20 percent of results.

If you worry about the extent of direct response knowledge, take heart. Brand advertising, which is most advertising you see, tends to disdain and ignore it. *Why* would make an article in its own right.

Advertising seeks to persuade. Direct response advertising does its best to play to proclivities. But neither can subvert will. None of this should surprise critical thinkers, who would likely scoff at a stage hypnotist making similar claims of mind control and manipulation.

Claim: Advertising contributes to social ills

There is an abundance of inoffensive advertising, but good apples do not preclude the existence of bad. One would be hard-pressed to name a societal ill that advertising hasn't promoted, piggybacked on, or tacitly endorsed. Circa 1907, a logo for Bluthenthal & Bickart's Alligator Bait whiskey featured a naked African American child tromping through a bayou. In 1957, Clairol began promoting hair coloring products with "Does she or doesn't she?" In 1965, "Mrs. Olson" began prescribing Folgers Coffee to women as a cure for the complaining husband. In 1967, Fritos introduced the Frito Bandito, an animated Mexican thief voiced by Mel Blanc whose mission in life was to steal your corn *cheeps*. In 2007, commercials for Haggar Clothing Company featured a pair of white, male, middle-aged spokesbrutes reveling in intolerance, bullying, vandalism, personal violence, and sexual harassment. In a 2008 TV commercial aired in the United Kingdom, Mr. T fired Snickers bars at a speed-walker to make him run "like a real man," closing with the tagline, "Get some nuts." As recently as 2014, DC Metro created posters suggesting that women would rather talk about shoes than think. Not to be overlooked are ads promoting products that harm the environment, threaten health, foster unwise debt, play upon greed, and more.

These are all valid charges leaving the advertising in question no place to hide. But here's a disturbing reminder: Greed, racism, sexism, cruel stereotypes, and other forms of marginalizing existed long before the first ad was penned. Advertising picks up, capitalizes on, and spreads ills, but it rarely authors them. When consciousness rises, advertising eventually follows. This is in no way a defense. When advertising perpetuates and, worse, promotes social ills, it deserves to be called on the carpet. But there is value in remembering that purging advertising of social ills begins with purging society of them.

As it is naive to pretend that advertising causes no harm, it is equally naive to pretend that it does no good. Advertising helps build and strengthen economies. If you have a job, it is thanks to people handing over dollars to your company, which is thanks to someone who persuaded them to do so, whether through an online banner, Twitter or Facebook mention, billboard, radio spot, brochure, magazine ad, or word-of-mouth. Mass advertising enables mass production, which lowers costs so that products can be made affordable and available where they wouldn't be otherwise. Trade, of which advertising and marketing are an integral part, helps keep nations from warring with one another. And, though I cannot speak for you, I am grateful that advertising has sometimes pushed what was once considered needless, like toothbrushes, daily bathing, and deodorant.

I would love to believe that intrinsic morality would prevent most advertising people from manipulating or controlling minds were such possible. Having seen many a lofty ideal dispatched where dollars were involved, I know better. So perhaps the most persuasive debunking of unfair persuasion techniques is that most practitioners do not bother with them. Equally telling is that, unlike consumer publications, advertising trade journals and how-to books do not bother with them, either.

What I dislike in advertising (not that you asked)

Crowing about nonexistent abuses may blind us to an abuse that is real and pervasive. I refer to a tactic that I consider immoral and at times dangerous. It is often overlooked, perhaps because it lacks sensationalistic appeal. It is called *lying*. I wish to draw attention to three kinds, two of them legal, one not.

Puffery is an exaggerated boast presumably understood not to be taken seriously. Surely few consumers believe that Keebler employs elves, Red Bull enables flight, and women cannot resist a man drenched in Axe body wash. You may differ, but I find puffery of that sort arguably harmless. Yet when Kellogg's puffed in the 1960s that Apple Jacks cereal "keeps the bullies away," I wonder how many kids consumed a bowl and went looking for trouble. And I disagree with a Fifth Circuit Court of Appeals ruling that allowed as puffery Papa John's Pizza's line, "better ingredients, better pizza," especially since the company's website calls the cagily incomplete comparative a "brand promise."

The other legally permissible lie is the *weasel*, and I have no tolerance for it. A weasel is technically true but designed to mislead. Fad diets weasel when they trumpet miracles disclaimed in tiny type as "not typical." So do multi-level companies that imply but do not explicitly claim that distributors are a few weeks from untold riches. So do natural and organic products that capitalize on the Appeal to Nature Fallacy. So do so-called alternative medicines, whose large type claims treatment and prevention while the small type offers the legally prescribed weasels, "These statements have not been evaluated by the FDA" and "This product is not intended to diagnose, treat, cure or prevent any disease."

Last on the list is *out-and-out lying*. There is nothing legal about it. How do no-goodniks get away with it? Some operate from a country that provides sanctuary. Some rightly expect regulatory bodies to be slow to action. Some keep operations local, knowing that the Federal Trade Commission pursues only interstate cases. Some hide their identity and close shop or move before the law catches up. Some count on projected profits to be greater than projected fines.

Wink or not at harmless puffery, but do not sit still for over-the-line puffery, weaseling, and out-and-out lying. Withhold your business. Warn friends. Blog. Send the offending advertiser angry mail. Write editors. Write legislators. Make a public stink.

Fair being fair, I'd also suggest rewarding honest advertisers with your business and public praise.

There is nothing an illicit advertiser would like better than to keep on bilking people under our noses while we tilt at mind-control windmills. Let's not.

Chapter 76

Ponytails and Prejudice

SOME YEARS AGO I hired a male account executive with a ponytail down to his lower back. I looked past the ponytail to find a smart, capable young executive, but it turned out that my clients did not. Reactions ranged from thinly veiled disdain, to comments made privately to me, to one jerk who openly mocked him to his face.

I had expected better.

At some level, most of us understand the importance of looking the part. We expect to see bankers in suits, nurses in scrubs, chefs in tall, silly white hats, pilots in uniforms, and the folks running the Disneyland Jungle Cruise in safari garb.

Drawing a fuzzy line separating understandable concerns from unfair ones is no easy matter. Besides anticipating clients' preferences and deciding which to indulge and which not to, employers must take care not to indulge their own prejudices by projecting them onto clients.

I have tended toward liberality in hiring and for the most part have been lucky, yet pragmatism reminds me that without clients one can stand on principle only for so long.

My ponytailed account executive bore the disdain with grace. My clients could have learned a thing or two from him.

Chapter 77

Marketing the Candidate

High school students complain that student body elections are naught but popularity contests. Fair enough. Look at who runs. Also, look at what's not at stake. Student body officers are not exactly in a position to lead a school into war or to economic ruin.

Now that we're grownups voting in national elections, we aren't dealing with popularity contests anymore.

That is, if we use our heads. Which largely we do not.

We humans like black-and-white. We have little patience for mottled hues, nuances, contingencies, histories, perspective, ins and outs, underlying factors, and agendas. We don't like being told that economies and international relations are chaotic and not perfectly predictable. We want decisive policies that can be summed up in sound bites.

In a world where nuanced, informed, thought-out answers do not fare well, one can hardly blame the candidates for oversimplifying issues and focusing on their respective brands instead.

"Focusing on their respective brands" is another way of saying "trying to get us to like them." Welcome back to high school.

This was driven home to me when I overheard myself say, "I suspect that I would personally dislike So-n-So, however, I support the greater part of So-n-So's platform, and I believe that So-n-So is a skillful politician who is likely to be effective." The statement was met with horror. *"How can you vote for someone you personally dislike?"* Never mind, apparently, the part about platform and effectiveness.

Much as I would love to rid politics of brand marketing, it cannot be done. You could try to do away with slick commercials, flatulent slogans, silly buttons, and stupid hats. You would most likely not succeed, but if you did, we would still have platforms, speaking style, well-honed sound bites, speeches, facial features, grooming, dress, gender, color, news show appearances (and also Fox News appearances), choices as to where to and not to stump, and more. All of these are elements of brand marketing, and they cannot be controlled.

Americans tend to choose candidates to whose image we respond most favorably. It is not unlike the way we choose a brand of peanut butter at the grocery store. We can do better. With an open mind and a bit of work, we can look past the brand, get a better handle on the nuances, and cast better informed votes.

I have ended up with the wrong peanut butter thanks to brand advertising. Ending up with the wrong elected official portends decidedly more.

Chapter 78

You Too Can Write Non-Sexist Copy

Bonus: If you're a good writer, you can do it without making your stuff awkward

My eighth grade English teacher *Mrs.* ("... no, no, no," she fumed, "not *Ms.* ...") Antoniazzi drilled into the class that in cases of unknown or mixed gender, we were to default to the use of masculine pronouns. Always.

That was the prevailing rule in 1968. (Yes, I am that old.) It no longer is, but plenty remain who bristle at having to approach gendered pronouns with care.

If you happen to be male, and odds are roughly 50/50 that you are, it's understandable if you don't quite get what the fuss is about. Slights and their sting often pass unnoticed by the non-slightee. Even slightees can be inured. More than once at the breakfast table in the early 70s, my stepmother, hopping-to ere Dad's coffee cup ran low, would spit out, "Women's lib! What do they need to be liberated from? Our first mistake was giving *them* the vote."

If you will not concede that women suffer negative effects from a default to masculine terms, I shall defer to Mrs. Antoniazzi, who told the unhappy girls in our class, "Rules are rules, and that's the rule." If rules are rules, then when rules change, so must we. This rule has changed. Defy it at the risk of being branded, not altogether unjustly, a sexist dinosaur.*

Many writers recoil at the awkwardness of the *his or her* construction. It is sometimes inevitable—I have used it in this volume—but it is too often the lazy writer's default. In most cases, you can do better with just a little bit of thought and skill. Here are some suggestions.

The Nix the Possessive Pronoun Technique: Instead of "everyone took his or her seat," how about "everyone took a seat."

The Find the Neuter Word Technique: Instead of "mankind" use "humankind." Instead of "workman" use "worker." Instead of "chairman" use "chair."

The Make It Plural Technique: Instead of "the customer likes his or her sandwich made fresh" you can say "customers like their sandwiches made fresh."

The Rewrite It Without a Possessive Technique: Instead of "the customer likes his or her sandwich made fresh" or "customers like their sandwiches made fresh," you could go with "customers like fresh-made sandwiches."

The Let Go of Your Favorite Cliché Technique: I don't care if you grew up saying *old wives' tale.* It is sexist and then some. Try *nonsense, untrue, fiddle-faddle, claptrap, questionable, baloney, myth, hogwash,* or *bull.* **

Ask the right person. Sexist expressions are good at taking writers unawares. It takes vigilance to recognize them and root them out. When in doubt, find a with-it, potential slightee and ask, "Is this wording sexist?" And don't argue with the answer.***

When in doubt, you're probably in doubt for good reason, so rewrite. You're in advertising. Creative solutions are what you're about.

Don't pout about having to do it. It's unbecoming.

* There is no shortage of ways to brand yourself a sexist dinosaur. A friend asked me to review an early draft of a marketing book he was writing. To illustrate the importance of incentive offers, he attempted a humorous take on the Old Testament story of Saul's offering a daughter to David as an incentive to kill Goliath. I advised my friend that joking about women being awarded as property was offensive. He retorted, "I hate that politically correct crap." Hate it he may, but readers who feel otherwise are free to express their ire by not buying his book and not retaining his services.

** When my goal is humor and irony, I go with *indeterminate-aged significant others' tale.*

*** Speaking of rewriting, I originally wrote that sentence, "Don't argue when they answer." But that didn't agree with the singular "slightee." And the last thing I wanted was "Don't argue when he or she answers."

Chapter 79

Businessmen: Shush Your Libido

Dear BusinessMAN:

I appreciated it when you sent a potential client my way, but I cringed when you added, "She's a hottie."

I'm not asking you not to be human, not to notice a pleasing appearance. I am asking you to keep the observation to yourself.

She is a professional. So am I. I intend to interact with her on that basis. When you tell me where she registers on your Personal Hotness Meter, you do her an injustice. You do me one, too. For that matter, you demean yourself.

This is the 21st Century. We have all had ample time to learn to do better.

Chapter 80

Lying to Sell a Legit Product Is Still Lying

Not for the first time, I just declined a potential client. Though there was nothing wrong with his product, everything was wrong with his sales pitch. It relied on sensationalized, exaggerated, flimflam health claims.

To be fair, I don't doubt that the fellow who called me believes every word of his pitch. That doesn't change the bogus nature of the claims.

A product sold by use of false or exaggerated claims cannot deliver the promised benefit. Even when there's nothing intrinsically wrong with the product, to promise what it cannot deliver is fraud.

Fraudulent claims separate the trusting from their money. That's immoral on its own merits. Fraudulent *health* claims add the serious, potential harm of lulling people into putting off real medical care. It can be life-threatening. Consider Apple founder Steve Jobs, who relied on "alternative care" until it was too late for real medicine to help.

If yours is a legitimate product that you're willing to sell without fibbing or exaggerating, even if it means selling less of it, call me. If you cannot or will not sell by being truthful, kindly lose my number.

Chapter 81

Of Belly-Button Lint and Bogus Ads

This piece was not for the trade press, but for Randi.org, the official website of the James Randi Educational Foundation (JREF). The JREF is a not-for-profit organization that debunks pseudoscientific and paranormal claims. The piece was for the most part well received, although a few readers accused me of being a shill.

Perhaps you have seen TV commercials for the so-called energy drink 5-Hour Energy. In one version, video and voiceover imply that for pepping up sleepy office workers, the product beats a cup of coffee. But bring your nose to the screen, and you'll see that the small type says the opposite: "Contains caffeine comparable to a cup of the leading coffee." Then, as the video segues to people enjoying improved physical performance, dexterity, and endurance, a new batch of small type says: "Not proven to improve physical performance, dexterity, or endurance." And, you'll read that the product "does not provide caloric energy." Interesting, since the energy that runs bodies is measured in calories.

Like many advertisers, the makers of 5-Hour Energy probably know they can safely and legally imply the bogus in large type as long as they properly disclaim it in small. In the industry this is known as a *weasel*: messaging that is technically accurate but designed to mislead.

Legislation can only do so much about weasels. While the ideal behind truth-in-advertising rules may be consumer protection, the reality is a kind of arms race wherein market-ers respond to new rules with an escalation of circumventive ingenuity.

Not that all marketers play that way. Abundant products and services are sold in a forthright manner and perform as promised. But this chapter isn't about good advertising prac-tices. It's about the other kind, and what we can do about them.

As a marketer who happens to be a skeptic and to have been cursed with a conscience, I have encountered and de-clined my share of earning opportunities with said other kind.

There was, for instance, the video producer who wanted me to script a TV commercial for a mineral which, when placed in a refrigerator, allegedly made food last longer. Intrigued, I asked if the product worked. "No," he said, "but that's what we're claiming." I sent him on his way.

There was the New Age enthusiast who claimed that her subliminal CDs helped people quit smoking, lose weight, save relationships, succeed-succeed-succeed, and, for all I know, make gravy without lumps. I could not advertise her CDs in good conscience. Telling her wasn't easy, not just because she believed in her product, and not just because my shop could have done with the work. We were about the same age, both single, and one of us (hint: not me) was quite attractive. I am not gifted in the flirtation department, but even I know bet-ter than to follow "Your product doesn't do what you think it does" with "Shall we go to dinner sometime?"

Other would-be clients that I declined include software that claims to but doesn't predict stock prices, a dial-an-astrologer company, a not-for-profit organization whose mission is the disenfranchisement of all who are not white, middle-aged, male, straight, right-wing, and aligned with its particular definition of "Christian," a weight-loss hypnotherapist, a pyramid scheme with a token product to keep it legal (aka multi-level marketing), and a neutraceuticals company whose products are neither nutritious nor ceutical ("ceutical" should be a word), to name a few.

None of this is to imply that I am any sort of paragon. I have allowed myself to be duped, and have even duped myself.

Before I knew better, I helped market a complement of antioxidant products trumpeting the manufacturer's myriad bogus health claims which I had accepted at face value.

I produced ads for a high-tech device in an established, legitimate category. Two years later, I learned that the manufacturer's PhD-level engineers had lied to me about their device's alleged technical superiority. In good faith, I had included their claims in the ads. I'm still mad.

And now I must come clean about the stock market software that I mentioned earlier. It purported to predict prices by use of technical analysis, the silly notion that you can impose scientific-looking mumbo-jumbo on a stock's past in order to reveal its future. The truth is, I didn't exactly decline them. I resigned them. They had been my client for years. During those years, did I believe for one minute that technical analysis worked? Hell no, and for good reason: It doesn't. But I rationalized. I told myself that as long as I didn't recruit new believers, it was OK to sell the software to existing ones. But the time came when I could no longer sell a product that didn't—couldn't—do as claimed, period. Worse, I realized that people who actually used the software risked more than the not insignificant purchase price. They risked gambling away everything they owned or had saved. Indeed, I later met an octogenarian who had wasted his considerable life savings, certain that each loss brought him closer to unlocking the secrets of predicting the stock market. Finally, unable to rationalize creating advertising for this awful product a moment longer, I resigned the account.

My favorite decline? Hermetically sealed belly-button lint. In fairness, this was not a flimflam product. I hadn't verified whether it truly was harvested from belly buttons, but I could see for myself that it was lint. The woman behind the idea believed that she had a novelty product in the tradition of the Pet Rock. I declined helping her market it for two reasons. One, I believed that it would not catch on, meaning that she would lose her money. Bad enough. Two, she wanted me to share in the cost, meaning that *I* would lose *my* money. Even worse.

I would love to tell you that by declining or resigning work, I have changed the world. Not so. The video producer found another writer, the so-called subliminal CDs went to market, the technical analysis software is still selling, you can still dial an astrologer, the right-wing public policy group still opposes rights for anyone not created in its own image, the weight-loss hypnotherapist is still making a great living not helping people lose weight, legal pyramid schemes are still flourishing, and neutraceuticals are still claiming in large type what they disclaim in small. And, for all I know, the would-be bellybutton lint magnate is still trying.

But at least I'm not helping. That's something.

Meanwhile, I do what I can. I write articles decrying false claims and weasels. To date, three respected marketing industry publications have run them. They even paid me for them. Doubly sweet. These publishers deserve credit for their courage, as scolding one's own readers and advertisers is a risky proposition.

You needn't write for marketing journals to make a difference. Individuals wield more power over marketers than many realize. The power resides largely in a secret weapon known as "the wallet." Marketers engage in tactics to make money. When enough people quit giving them money, marketers must change tactics or go out of business. No legislature forced the Coca-Cola Company to replace New Coke with Coke Classic. Old-fashioned pressure from ordinary, wallet-wielding, impassioned people took care of that.

So when you observe an objectionable marketing tactic, I would suggest for starters avoiding rewarding unethical marketers. You do this by not buying the product.

To go one better, tell your friends you're refusing to buy, and why. Post on Facebook. Start a Facebook group. Tweet. If you have a blog, blog. Marketers have great respect for The Power of Word of Mouth, as well they should. Generate enough public snark, and they will take note. And, on occasion, action.

If you like to write, research your case and then compose letters stating it well. Send them to editors. Letters that present a well-defended case stand a good chance of publication. While you're at it, send them to the managers of publications, networks, and stations that run the offending ads, as well as to the producers of programs the ads sponsor.

Emails are good and are gaining in power, but do not overlook the power of snail mail. Right or wrong, businesspeople tend to think you're more serious and more statistically significant when you go to the trouble of signing a letter, placing it in an envelope, affixing a stamp, and dropping it in a mailbox.

You might also send a letter to the person ultimately responsible for creating the marketing in the first place. It's a long shot, but who knows? Early in my career, I received an angry letter from a reader who had taken offense at an inadvertent stereotype in an ad I'd approved. Theretofore oblivious, I saw the unintended slight the moment she pointed it out, pulled the ad, and sent her a letter of apology and thanks.

My glasses aren't so rose-colored as for me to suggest, much less believe, that by these actions we will stop unsavory marketing practices cold. But let's not sell short the cumulative power of individual efforts. Marketing history brims with cases where a tidal wave of individual efforts forced mighty companies to change course. An accumulation of individual efforts pushed Capitol Records to change the cover of a Beatles LP, McDonald's to stop cooking fries in animal fat (the second time around, that is), Chrysler to stop resetting odometers to zero after test drives, Cadbury New Zealand to stop adding palm oil to milk chocolate, the Direct Marketing Association to create a Do-Not-Mail registry, food manufacturers to cut back on sugars, Apple to make good on iPhone antenna problems, and more. And in addition to efforts by the JREF and other organizations, the sheer volume of outcry from individuals had much to do with reforming ridiculous libel laws in the UK.

Short of such dramatic results, there is something to be said for the satisfaction of knowing one is doing what one can.

The whole idea behind a market-driven economy is that the market does the driving. We are the market. Let's retake the wheel.

Chapter 82

Why I Am for PC Speech, Caveats Notwithstanding

SOME YEARS AGO it was my misfortune to be acquainted with a 20-year-old who, often in front of his mother, used "you woman" as an insult directed at men. I asked him, in front of his mother, "I believe your mom is a woman. How is that an insult?" By way of reply, he invited me to engage myself in sexual intercourse. I understood him better when, years later, I happened upon a book about psychopathy. Of the 10 symptoms the authors listed, he displayed 15.

As for us non-psychopaths, most of us prefer not to say hurtful things when we needn't. That's why we train our children not to point and bellow, "That person is fat." It's why we're mortified when the wrong person overhears what was intended as a private remark.

We call that kind of consideration *manners* and *common decency*. Were it not for the negative connotation, we might equally call it *political correctness*. But the negative connotation exists and, as connotations go, this one is powerful. It is not a little ironic that in some circles political correctness is treated as politically incorrect.

The negative connotation is not terribly hard to understand. For one thing, none of us likes to be corrected. The less kind the correction, the less we like it. For another, while the offense of "that person is fat" is universally understood, it's not so easy to understand why a word with a history of acceptability is suddenly to be avoided the moment a once-silent group suddenly says, "We don't like that." Nor is it easy to understand the need to abandon a once-acceptable term when it begins to take on a new, unacceptable meaning. Here it is important not to fall prey to the Genetic Fallacy, that of holding to what a word once meant but no longer means. These days it's not a good idea to refer to laymen as *idiots*. On the other hand, the former ethnic slur *Samaritan* has become quite the compliment.

Yet attention to the effect of words on people coming from a different frame of reference moves society, albeit sometimes kicking and screaming, in a positive direction. Empathy, the art of identifying with what's going on in someone else's head, is a worthy talent to acquire and grow.

To be sure, sometimes PC speech is carried too far. Sometimes it is used to bully. Sometimes it is ambiguous, deceptive, excessively euphemistic. These are not arguments against PC speech but against extremes.

The usual objections to PC speech do not hold up well. Take the fellow I know who frowned and lamented, "It's getting to the point where you can't disparage any group anymore." That's a bad thing? Or another who told me he resented having to "think so much" before opening his mouth. That, too, is a bad thing? Take my friends who, when I pointed out that a certain phrase was in fact a racial slur, apologized and pledged never again to use it. Ha, ha, just kidding. They launched into a diatribe about how "They" shouldn't be so sensitive. Why not "We" shouldn't be so *in*sensitive? Or take those who reply, "lighten up," "it was just a joke," or "you don't have to get so upset about it." These knee-jerk defenses born of wounded pride are understandable, but they need to go. The more constructive reaction is to pause, think, and, where needed, apologize and make a mental note to do better.

I recall being corrected, not kindly, upon using what I hadn't known was a sexist term. To add to my humiliation, the colleague doing the correcting disliked me (which went both ways) and sought at every turn to sabotage my career (which did not). Trouble is, her correcting me was called for, and I have avoided the term ever since. I contented myself with finding other reasons not to like her, which abounded.

Chapter 83

On Morality in Marketing

My hat is off to the advertising industry trade publications Deliver *and* Direct Marketing IQ *for running, respectively, the articles that became this and the next chapter. They risked offending readers and advertisers alike.*

In my column for a consumer publication, I wrote:

> If you bought a car you can't afford, fed your kids fast food until your spouse mistook them for the minivan, blew the budget on a video game system, or bought clothes that went out of style as you were paying for them, I'm truly sorry. But neither my marketing colleagues nor I made you do it.

I intended the article to be an empowering piece on personal responsibility, and to bust a few myths about marketing's alleged powers of mind control. But some readers recoiled, taking it for a unilateral defense of marketing, abuses included, and a disavowal of marketers' responsibilities for what and how they sell.

Fair is fair. Insisting that our markets accept responsibility for their buying decisions in no way relieves us marketers of responsibility for how we use our marketing knowledge.

Marketing knowledge itself is neutral. Knowing what kind of link people are more likely to click does not make it immoral to use that kind of link, nor does knowing the power of limited-time incentive offers make limited-time incentive offers underhanded. It is in *how* we put our knowledge to use that abuses can and do occur.

To be sure, much if not the majority of today's marketing is forthright and honorable. But too much resorts, if not to out-and-out lies, to stating what is technically true in a manner designed to mislead. Don't believe me? Consider products that make fantastic claims in body copy that the fly type contradicts.

An early commercial for 5-Hour Energy did just that. While the video and voiceover implied that a so-called "energy product" beat a cup of coffee for helping sleepy workers slog through an afternoon, onscreen fly type revealed the secret ingredient to be—guess what?—"… caffeine comparable to a cup of the leading coffee." Not only that. The product shown making people alert and productive was "… not proven to improve physical performance, dexterity, or endurance." For that matter, it "… does not provide caloric energy." That's interesting, since the energy that bodies run on is measured in calories. What is not caloric is not energy.

Some marketers justify subterfuges with, "Our customers are intelligent people who research our claims." That bit of nonsense is *caveat emptor* in a new suit of clothes. Nor can we count on the oft-quoted maxim that "effective advertising only speeds a bad product's demise" to weed out abuses. For just one example, consider magnets with purported health benefits. Blinded tests show no therapeutic effect, a Federal District Court ordered one magnet marketer to refund up to $87,000,000 to defrauded buyers, and the iron in our blood doesn't respond to magnets. Yet millions of people continue believing in and buying so-called "therapeutic magnets." Effective marketing has built, not killed, this flimflam product.

Hopefully you agree that out-and-out deceptive practices are harmful. Short of extremes, varying shades of gray require judgment calls. As David Ogilvy wrote in *Confessions of an Advertising Man*, "Surely it is asking too much to expect an advertiser to describe the shortcomings of his product. One must be forgiven for putting one's best foot forward." Fair enough. Were full disclosure required in every exchange, most of us would never have had a first date.

While we can expect disagreement as to when putting one's best foot forward becomes misrepresentation, engaging in the dialog beats failing to deal with the issue at all. But when it comes to darkest gray areas, we would do well to self-police. If the idea of higher moral ground fails to motivate, perhaps the prospect of obviating needlessly and overly restrictive laws will do the trick.

Kudos to marketers who, at one end of the spectrum, showcase real benefits and sell legitimate products. Raspberries to those who, at the other end, resort to the weasel known as "technically true enough not to be illegal."

Chapter 84

Drawing the Proverbial Line

Accustomed to a recent clinical study, hiring my agency reduces your risk of getting cancer.

I conducted the study myself. It's poorly designed, shamelessly biased and wholly unscientific, but that doesn't mean I can't slap words like "clinical" and "study" on it. And though I'm no attorney, I'm pretty sure that with carefully chosen weasels and the right disclaimers, I can use it to relieve the gullible of cash while I avoid fines and jail.

Put down your pitchforks and torches. I'm not serious about offering my shop as a cancer preventative. I am, however, quite serious about the fact that I could easily abuse "clinical study" were I so inclined, and in general about the ease with which one can mislead while remaining technically within the law.

If you work in marketing, you may someday be asked to execute just such a strategy. What course will you choose?

I hope and suspect that most readers would decline products that rely on blatantly false claims like "Take this pill tonight and wake up a millionaire tomorrow." I think most would also dismiss as foolhardy anyone who insists on full, unvarnished disclosure, like "Our cologne smells good, but, face it, nothing short of overhauling your looks and personality will get you a date, and you might also consider bathing while you're at it." The dilemmas lurk in-between, in those darned shades of gray.

It doesn't help that each shade is only slightly lighter or darker than its neighbor. One person's "OK" may be another's "not OK." I recently declined a prospective client whose product was popular, legal, and backed by testimonials from happy customers. I turned it down because blinded tests showed the product did not deliver the promised benefit. Not a few colleagues accused me of being too stringent. If customers are happy, they argued, no harm done. Obviously, they and I disagree.

I allow that how much or how little gray you'll abide is your decision, not mine. What's important is to draw that proverbial line, and to draw it well before you need to refer to it. Ethical challenges seem never to come along when declining work is convenient. One well-funded company had a habit of reappearing and asking me to reconsider taking on their flim-flam product at times my shop needed business most.

Not everyone agrees that marketers bear responsibility for what and how they sell. The prospective buyer, they say, is free to check facts. The term that best characterizes that defense also refers to a bovine by-product useful for fertilizing lawns and gardens. Search the how-to literature of marketing. It brims with advice on building credibility, winning trust, and giving readers useful information. We cannot work to win the market's trust, urge them to buy, and then call it their fault when they do.

As you ponder which products to accept or decline and which tactics to embrace or reject, here are some points to consider:

Does the small type contradict the large? Not all fly type is underhanded. Much of it is useful and appropriate or meets a legal requirement, silly or not. But when what's buried in small type is the antithesis of what's conveyed in large, it suggests something about the overall integrity of the piece. Not to mention of the advertiser.

How many weasels will you indulge? Here's a revealing exercise: count the use of terms like "may," "can," "believed to," "said to," "no claim is made," "not evaluated by," "not intended to," "not typical," "may vary," "not verified by," and so forth. See if the total falls within your personal limit.

Get real. Come on. You know when "results may vary" means "works nine out of ten times in properly conducted, controlled tests" and when it means "works no better than you'd expect from random chance."

Does evidence back the claim? If your client and one million passionate customers assert but cannot demonstrate a claim, on-demand and repeatedly, you have testimonials but not evidence. Given the power of testimonials, that's good reason to check the evidence before using them.

Beware data in the hands of fools. It's remarkably easy to make numbers support just about any position. I recommend Darrell Huff's short but excellent *How to Lie with Statistics*. Published in 1954, it's still popular and easy to find.

Do you use the product? Does the client? I find it telling that none of the employees of a get-rich-quick software company use or own the product. Not even the folks who are great at selling it over the phone use it. Seems to me that if the product delivered on its get-rich-quick promise, all of the company's employees would have used it and be basking in untold riches instead of continuing to work for wages.

Would you recommend the product to your kids? How about to your aging, fixed-income parents? If you are squeamish about foisting a product on a loved one, you are squeamish about the product.

Most marketing is above-board and honorable. But I'm painfully aware, as I'm sure you are, of glaring exceptions. I hold no delusion that my whining here, or that our drawing proverbial lines, will bring such practices to an end. But there's no need for you and me to take part in them.

Chapter 85

The Sometimes High Cost of Integrity

Not long ago at a convention I met a man who had just abandoned his profession of 16 years. This was no mere case of finding a new job, itself not a small matter, but of finding a new career. It meant he would not be using the advanced degree he had worked so hard to obtain. And it meant giving up a solid income, community status, and considerable professional recognition.

He made this drastic change after coming to realize that his field did not and could not deliver what it promised in return for people's money.

To utter "I was wrong" is difficult enough for any human with an ego, which is any human. When uttering "I was wrong" means giving up a successful career, it can be all but impossible.

To be sure, many people who work for a questionable organization or market a questionable product do so unawares. No reason to question, much less dig deep, may ever have occurred to them. And not a few have been indoctrinated to the point of being fierce defenders.

But not all are innocent. Some knowingly peddle flim-flam products or misrepresent marginal ones and don't give a damn about it. They hide behind *caveat emptor*, as if resorting to a heinous cliché to rationalize ripping people off is okay provided you say the heinous cliché in Latin.

I feel for those who, having begun to suspect that all is not well, are stewing over what to do about it. To resign a client whose products don't perform as claimed is one thing; to resign your whole career is quite another.

More than once, I have wondered if I could have done what the fellow I met at the convention did. His willingness to examine and weigh facts was no small thing. His acknowledging where the facts led was bigger. That he felt he no choice but to change careers? Huge.

Chapter 86

Weasel, Weasel, Weasel

I just listened to a radio spot for Arrowhead Brand Mountain Spring Water, and I'm upset. The essence of the spot is that all water may *look* the same, but since Arrowhead comes from springs that aren't the same springs that Arrowhead's competitors get their water from, well, the folks at Arrowhead "believe" that their water is better, and they "believe" that you will taste the difference, too.

Used in this way, "believe" is what the advertising industry calls a *weasel*. It sounds like a claim, but upon examination you realize that they aren't quite saying what it sounds like they're saying. They carefully avoid out-and-out claiming that their water tastes better. If they made a statement like that, they would need to be prepared to back it up. So they tell you what they *believe* and what they *think that* you will *believe*. That way, there's nothing to prove. It keeps them legally safe.

Now, it's conceivable Arrowhead water indeed has a distinct taste advantage. If it has, all it would take to establish as much is a controlled, triple-blinded test conducted by a neutral third party. The fact that Arrowhead chooses to weasel instead suggests that they are counting on suggestion. And you can bet that they won't be disappointed. A number of people hearing or reading Arrowhead's tripe, upon sampling the water, are apt to convince themselves that Arrowhead really does taste lots better than other water.

Such practices help give advertising and advertisers a bad name. As if we need help doing that.

Minerals aside, water is water, a parity product. There's nothing wrong with parity products, and there are ways to sell them without weaseling.

Chapter 87

The Trouble with "Results May Vary"

Advertising Age reported in 2009 that new regulations might no longer allow diet plans and fitness equipment advertisers to use weasels like "experience may vary" and "results not typical." Readers lost no time condemning government in the comments section of the online edition. Not me. Here is the comment I posted.

S orry, folks. I'm on the government's side. I own a direct response shop. It has long troubled me that many in my industry use misleading advertising to promote questionable products.

Take diet plans. If 99 percent of your ad promises miracles and one percent says "results may vary" or "results not typical," the ad is 99 percent misleading, and you know it. You also know—read your fine print—that no plan works without diet and exercise. Trouble is, diet and exercise work *without* the plan. You are taking money for a product that has the same effect whether customers use it or not.

Take natural remedies. If your product contains only natural ingredients, you can *imply* that it helps with myriad symptoms provided your fly type contains statements like "these claims have not been evaluated by the FDA" and "not intended to treat or cure any disease." Wait a sec. Isn't treating or curing what the rest of the ad is about? If 99 percent of your ad claims miracles and 1 percent disclaims them, the ad is 99 percent misleading, and you know it.

Your files may burst with testimonials. You may use the product and believe in it. Irrelevant. Millions of Americans believe the lunar landing was faked, that George W. Bush engineered the events of 9/11, and that vaccines cause autism. Neither their numbers nor their passion makes them right.

Nor am I impressed with your "clinical studies." If I wanted to, I could come up with a clinical study suggesting that hiring my agency "may help relieve arthritis pains" and, given the right disclaimers, quite possibly get away with it.

Some allege that no harm exists in marketing that is 99 percent misleading. After all, some people lose weight on the diet plans, and some derive a placebo effect from worthless remedies. Here's the harm: (1) People with serious weight and/or health issues risk, to their ultimate harm, delaying real treatment while they try your flimflam preparation. (2) Some natural remedies that do not perform as claimed *are still drugs* and can have undesired effects, including interfering with legitimate medications. (3) Deliberately misleading is a de facto immoral practice. (4) You hurt the image of the marketers who don't stoop to such levels. (5) You hurt the industry by bringing regulators down upon us all.

If marketers would self-police, the FTC wouldn't need to get involved. Please, marketers, resolve never to take on a product that you can't sell by telling the truth. The resolve would help you, the industry, and people at large.

Chapter 88

Responsible Use of Color

As you might expect, a piece from a dentist in this morning's mail featured photos of beautiful people with perfect smiles. Yet something was missing. Namely, people who weren't Caucasian.

Non-Caucasians account for more than a third of our nation's population. And to the best of my knowledge, not just Caucasians grow teeth.

Curious, I grabbed two national, mass-circulation magazines and counted the photos and illustrations with people in them. In one, a news magazine, 71 percent of ads with people photos showed only whites, seven percent showed only non-whites, and 22 percent showed both. The other, a general interest magazine, was less encouraging. In every ad with a photo of people, the photo was of white people only. Period.

Next, I piled all of the past few days' worth of direct mail, most of it from national advertisers, on my desk. I found that 89 percent showed white people only, six percent showed non-whites only, and five percent showed both.

These data are non-scientific, but they are suggestive and disconcerting. Purely from a marketing standpoint, an advertiser who depicts customers of just one race risks losing sales, since those who are excluded may fail to identify with the ads or, worse, take offense. But the concern runs deeper from a human standpoint. Our ability to sort by physical characteristics is useful for mushroomers who wish to avoid poisoning themselves, children who need to keep family members straight from strangers, and dog owners who don't want to leave the park with the wrong dog. The problem is in a side effect wherein we tend to separate into "us" and "them."

Decades ago, hippie-era youth sang about filling the world with love, buying it a Coke, and treating one another as brothers and sisters. Today, science backs ideology by attesting to the "brothers and sisters" part. Mitochondrial DNA shows that any two people from any two points on the globe share common ancestors. It also shows that there are more genetic differences between people within a population than between two different populations overall.

To be mercenary about it, advertising that is more inclusive will appeal to more people, so inclusiveness may help you sell more of your products. Beyond that and more important, advertisers have a powerful opportunity to reinforce the fact that humankind really is one vast family. Let's not waste the opportunity.

I doubt that the dentist intended to slight. Everyone could do with the occasional reminder. I hope this serves.

Chapter 89

Ethical Marketing vs. Not-So-Ethical Marketing

The genesis of this brief piece was a note from a colleague asking for my definition of ethical selling.

Ethical selling aligns people with what they want or need. That it helps build a strong economy in the process is a convenient side benefit.

Not all selling is ethical. Browbeating, misrepresenting, out-and-out lying, and various forms of manipulation are all too common. Consider: sellers of big ticket items who con the inexperienced into spending more than is needful or wise; salespeople who guilt, shame, or harass the timid; flimflammers like Kevin Trudeau; and even your garden variety TV evangelist.

It gets murky when the public demands what's legal but harmful, such as tobacco products, or what's legal but doesn't perform as claimed, such as most multi-level marketing firms, so-called alternative "medicines" or "therapies," psychic hotlines, software purporting to predict stock prices, and so forth.

A marketer with a conscience will sooner or later end up declining taking on a client or product and, with it, decline an opportunity to make money.

Acknowledgments

I am indebted to my first editor, *The Sparks Tribune*'s Lynn Woodward, who engaged me to write a weekly column when I was 15. I am also grateful to later editors who regularly requested and published my work: Dan Grantham, Lori Bremerkamp, and Darrell Dawsey, all of *Deliver* magazine; Barry Karr and Kendrick Frazier of *Skeptical Inquirer*; Ethan Bolt of *DirectMarektingIQ*; Ann Handley of *MarketingProfs.com*; and Susen Sawatski of *Adnews*.

I owe heartfelt thanks to "Miss Kitt" Bradley, Michael Hartwell, Ryan Jackson (who happens to be my nephew, poor guy), and long-time friend and associate Jeff Bacon for poring over the manuscript and pruning it of myriad typos and other embarrassments. I produce more mistakes than anyone could possibly find, so if you happen upon more, please blame me and not them.

About Steve Cuno

Steve landed his first paid writing gig at 15 when *The Sparks Tribune*, a northern Nevada community newspaper, started a weekly tabloid for high school students. He received $5 per column. That was in the days when you could buy a paperback novel for 50 cents and a hammered but drivable used car for two hundred dollars. He lost no time in finding his writer's voice and hasn't shut up since.

Steve worked for a number of years in branding and direct response advertising on the client and agency sides. He opened the RESPONSE Agency in 1994.

In his spare time, Steve likes to read, walk his dog, pound away on his piano, and force people to look at photos of his grandchildren, holding them against their will until they concede that no one else's are as cute.

ALSO BY STEVE CUNO

*Prove It Before You Promote It:
How to Take the Guesswork Out
of Advertising*

*The RESPONSE Agency Guide
to Direct Mail*

BY JOANNE HANKS
AS TOLD TO STEVE CUNO

*It's Not About the Sex My Ass:
Confessions of an Ex-Mormon,
Ex-Polygamist, Ex-Wife*

www.ingramcontent.com/pod-product-compliance
Lightning Source LLC
Chambersburg PA
CBHW020730180526
45163CB00001B/180